AVERY LOCKE

C 12 Microservices Architecture With .NET 8

Advanced Tech

Contents

Introduction

The rise of **microservices architecture** has transformed how modern applications are built and maintained. In today's software development landscape, developers and organizations are moving away from traditional monolithic structures to distributed, cloud-native systems. This shift has been driven by the need for scalability, flexibility, and efficiency in delivering applications that can keep up with ever-growing business demands. For developers working with **C# 12** and **.NET 8**, the opportunity to adopt and master microservices is more compelling than ever.

This introduction will walk you through the concept of **microservices**, explore the evolution from **monolithic** architectures, and explain the numerous benefits and challenges microservices bring to the table. We will also dive into the advantages of using **C# 12** and **.NET 8** for building microservices, highlighting their latest features that streamline the process. Finally, we'll provide an overview of **cloud-native** and **distributed systems**—key components in the microservices ecosystem—and explain the structure of this book and how to use it to unlock the full potential of microservices with .NET 8.

What Are Microservices?

At its core, **microservices architecture** is an approach to software development that structures an application as a collection of loosely coupled, independently deployable services. Each service in a microservice architecture performs a specific function and communicates with other services over standard protocols, typically through a lightweight API (often REST or gRPC). This modularity allows for flexibility, scalability, and ease of maintenance, making microservices a preferred choice for complex, large-scale applications.

Key Characteristics of Microservices:

- **Autonomy**: Each microservice operates independently, meaning it can be developed, deployed, and scaled without affecting the rest of the system.
- **Decentralized Data Management**: Unlike monolithic architectures, microservices often have their own databases and manage their own data, reducing dependencies between services.
- **Focused on Specific Business Capabilities**: Microservices are typically aligned with specific business functions, which makes it easier to update, maintain, and extend functionalities without disrupting the entire application.
- **Technology Agnostic**: Different microservices can be built using different programming languages or technologies, allowing teams to choose the best tools for specific tasks.
- **Resilience**: Microservices promote fault tolerance. Since services are loosely coupled, failure in one service does not necessarily bring down the entire application.

Examples of Microservices in the Real World

- **E-commerce Platforms**: E-commerce platforms like **Amazon** use microservices to handle various functions such as inventory management,

2

payment processing, and user authentication. Each of these functions can be updated or scaled independently.

- **Streaming Services**: Platforms like **Netflix** utilize microservices to manage user profiles, content recommendations, streaming quality, and billing. This allows Netflix to deploy changes or improvements without affecting the entire service.
- **Banking Systems**: Banks use microservices to manage transactions, customer profiles, fraud detection, and notifications, which allows for faster development cycles and improved security measures.

Evolution from Monolithic to Microservices

What is a Monolithic Architecture?

Before microservices, **monolithic architectures** were the dominant model for building software applications. In a monolithic system, all of the application's components are tightly integrated into a single, unified codebase. This means that the user interface (UI), server-side logic, and database interactions are all part of one large, interdependent system.

Monolithic applications work well for smaller, less complex applications where the entire codebase can be managed by a single team. However, as applications grow in size and complexity, monolithic architectures become more challenging to maintain. Even small changes to one part of the application can require redeploying the entire system, leading to longer development cycles and increased risk of introducing bugs.

The Drawbacks of Monolithic Architectures

- **Scaling Issues**: Monolithic applications are difficult to scale because they require the entire application to be scaled, even if only a single component is under heavy load.
- **Slower Development Cycles**: As the codebase grows, it becomes more difficult for developers to understand the entire system, leading to slower development and more frequent bugs.
- **Tightly Coupled Dependencies**: Since all components are interde-

3

pendent, a change in one area of the system can lead to unintended consequences in other areas, increasing the risk of errors and failures.

- **Limited Technology Stack Flexibility**: With monolithic applications, all components must use the same technology stack, which limits the flexibility of choosing the best tools for specific parts of the system.

The Transition to Microservices

The transition from monolithic to microservices architecture was driven by the need to address the limitations of monolithic applications. Organizations realized that decoupling different parts of their systems could improve scalability, increase flexibility, and reduce development time. Microservices allow each component of the application to be developed, deployed, and maintained independently, which leads to shorter development cycles and greater resilience.

The move toward **cloud computing** and **distributed systems** further accelerated the adoption of microservices, as cloud environments are inherently scalable and provide the perfect infrastructure for microservices deployment. With microservices, organizations could fully leverage the benefits of cloud environments by deploying individual services on different servers, regions, or even clouds, leading to greater redundancy, performance, and cost-efficiency.

Benefits and Challenges of Microservices Architecture

Benefits of Microservices

1. **Scalability** Microservices can be scaled independently, meaning that only the parts of the system experiencing heavy demand need to be scaled. This leads to more efficient use of resources and cost savings, as compared to monolithic architectures that require the entire application to be scaled.

2. **Faster Development Cycles** Since microservices are loosely coupled, different teams can work on different services without worrying about

interfering with each other's work. This parallel development leads to shorter release cycles and faster time to market.

3. **Fault Isolation and Resilience** In a microservices architecture, the failure of one service doesn't necessarily affect the entire system. This isolation of faults improves the overall resilience of the system and makes it easier to identify and fix problems.

4. **Technology Flexibility** Microservices allow developers to choose the right tools for the job. For example, one service could be written in C#12 while another might use Python, depending on the team's preferences and the requirements of the service.

5. **Easier Maintenance and Updates** Updating a microservice is simpler and less risky than updating a monolithic application because the changes are isolated to a single service. This reduces the chance of introducing bugs that affect the entire system.

6. **Improved Team Autonomy** Microservices empower teams to take full ownership of the services they build, including development, deployment, and maintenance. This autonomy increases team productivity and reduces bottlenecks in the development process.

Challenges of Microservices

1. **Complexity in System Design** Microservices architectures are more complex to design than monolithic architectures. Developers need to carefully consider service boundaries, communication protocols, and data consistency. Poorly designed microservices can lead to inefficiencies and difficult-to-maintain systems.

2. **Inter-Service Communication** Since microservices communicate with each other over the network, there is an added layer of complexity in managing inter-service communication. Issues such as latency, network failures, and communication timeouts must be handled carefully.

3. **Data Consistency** In a distributed microservices architecture, maintaining data consistency across services can be a challenge. Developers

need to design systems that can handle eventual consistency, distributed transactions, or employ event-driven patterns to manage state changes across services.

4. **Deployment and Monitoring Overheads** While microservices enable frequent deployments, the overhead associated with deploying and monitoring multiple services can be significant. Setting up proper continuous integration/continuous deployment (CI/CD) pipelines, logging, and monitoring systems requires careful planning and infrastructure.

5. **Security Concerns** With microservices, security becomes more complex as each service must be independently secured. This often requires implementing additional layers of authentication, authorization, and encryption to ensure secure communication between services.

6. **Debugging and Testing** Debugging and testing microservices are more difficult than in monolithic applications because services run independently and communicate over the network. Developers need to employ new strategies, such as distributed tracing, to diagnose issues across multiple services.

Why C#12 and .NET 8 for Microservices?

The choice of **C#12** and **.NET 8** for building microservices brings numerous advantages to the table, thanks to the latest enhancements in these technologies. Microsoft's commitment to cloud-native development, performance optimization, and seamless integration with popular cloud platforms makes .NET 8 the ideal framework for building microservices, while C#12 introduces powerful new features that improve developer productivity and code quality.

Key Advantages of C#12 for Microservices:

- **Enhanced Asynchronous Programming**: C#12 continues to build on its robust support for asynchronous programming with improvements in async and await. This is critical in microservices architectures where handling concurrency and I/O-bound operations efficiently is essential.

- **Source Generators**: Source generators, introduced in C#9 and enhanced in later versions, allow developers to generate code during compilation. This is especially useful in microservices where repetitive code (like API client generation) can be automated.
- **Pattern Matching and Record Types**: The expanded pattern matching and record types in C#12 help developers write cleaner, more readable code, making it easier to maintain and refactor microservices.

Why .NET 8 is Ideal for Microservices:

- **Performance and Efficiency**: .NET 8 introduces performance improvements in areas like memory management, garbage collection, and async operations, making it well-suited for high-performance microservices that need to handle many requests concurrently.
- **Cross-Platform Support**: .NET

8 offers seamless cross-platform support, enabling microservices to be deployed on various platforms, including Windows, Linux, and macOS, without additional configuration.

- **Cloud-Native Integration**: .NET 8 is designed with cloud-native applications in mind, offering built-in support for containerization (through Docker), orchestration (with Kubernetes), and serverless computing (via Azure Functions and AWS Lambda).
- **Minimal APIs**: Minimal APIs in .NET 8 simplify the creation of lightweight microservices by reducing the boilerplate code required to set up an API, making it easier to start small services quickly.

With these features, **C#12** and **.NET 8** provide a robust foundation for building modern, scalable, and high-performing microservices.

Overview of Cloud-Native and Distributed Systems

A core tenet of microservices architecture is its compatibility with **cloud-native** and **distributed systems**. These systems leverage the power of cloud platforms and distributed computing to scale and maintain applications in real-time.

What Are Cloud-Native Systems?

Cloud-native systems are applications designed to run in cloud environments, making the most of the cloud's scalability, flexibility, and reliability. Cloud-native applications are typically built using microservices architectures and leverage containerization, orchestration, and serverless technologies.

Key components of cloud-native systems include:

- **Containers (e.g., Docker)**: Containers allow microservices to be packaged along with their dependencies and deployed consistently across environments.
- **Orchestration (e.g., Kubernetes)**: Orchestration platforms like Kubernetes automate the deployment, scaling, and management of containerized applications.
- **Serverless Computing (e.g., Azure Functions)**: Serverless platforms abstract the infrastructure management, allowing developers to focus on writing code while the cloud provider handles the scaling and execution of the microservices.

Distributed Systems and Microservices

A **distributed system** consists of multiple, independent components (or nodes) that communicate and coordinate to achieve a common goal. Microservices architecture is inherently a distributed system, as each microservice runs independently but needs to interact with other services.

Distributed systems offer several advantages:

- **Scalability**: Distributed systems can scale horizontally by adding more

nodes to handle increased loads.
- **Fault Tolerance**: If one node fails, the system can continue functioning by rerouting traffic or recovering from the failure.
- **Geographical Distribution**: Services can be distributed across different regions to reduce latency and improve performance for users in different locations.

However, building distributed systems also introduces challenges, such as maintaining data consistency, handling network failures, and managing inter-service communication.

Book Structure and How to Use This Guide

This book is designed to take you on a journey through the world of **microservices architecture** using **C#12** and **.NET 8**. Whether you are a seasoned developer looking to expand your knowledge or a beginner eager to dive into microservices, this guide will provide you with the tools and understanding needed to build, deploy, and maintain high-performing microservices applications.

How This Book is Structured:

- **Chapter 1-2**: We'll start with the basics of microservices architecture, including setting up your development environment and creating your first microservice.
- **Chapter 3-7**: You'll then explore core concepts like microservices design patterns, advanced C#12 features, and inter-service communication.
- **Chapter 8-12**: These chapters will dive into the complexities of deploying microservices to the cloud, monitoring and scaling them, and ensuring resilience and fault tolerance.
- **Chapter 13-14**: You'll discover cutting-edge trends and future innovations in microservices, including serverless computing and integrating AI/ML into your services.
- **Chapter 15**: Finally, we'll walk through an end-to-end case study,

applying everything learned throughout the book to build and deploy a complete microservices architecture.

How to Use This Guide:

Each chapter is designed to stand on its own, allowing you to dive into specific topics that interest you or follow along from start to finish. You'll find hands-on examples, code snippets, and best practices that will guide you through every aspect of building microservices with C#12 and .NET 8.

By the end of this book, you'll have a deep understanding of microservices architecture and the skills necessary to build scalable, secure, and resilient applications using modern tools and frameworks.

Chapter 1: Getting Started with Microservices Architecture

Microservices architecture has revolutionized the way modern applications are designed, developed, and deployed. As businesses and developers move away from monolithic systems, microservices offer a way to build more scalable, flexible, and maintainable applications. In this chapter, we will lay the foundation for building microservices using C#12 and .NET 8 by exploring key microservices design principles and setting up your development environment.

We will begin with an in-depth look at microservices design principles, focusing on concepts like **Single Responsibility**, **Decoupling**, **Scalability**, and **Fault Tolerance**. Next, we'll walk through setting up your development environment, including installing .NET 8 SDK and configuring IDEs such as Visual Studio and VS Code. Finally, we will introduce **Docker** and **containerization**, critical tools in deploying microservices efficiently.

Understanding Microservices Design Principles

Microservices architecture hinges on a set of well-defined design principles that guide the creation and operation of microservices. These principles ensure that microservices remain scalable, maintainable, and loosely coupled, offering maximum flexibility for deployment and updates.

1. Single Responsibility Principle

One of the core tenets of microservices is the **Single Responsibility Principle** (SRP). This principle states that a service should have only one reason to change—meaning each microservice should be responsible for a single, well-defined business function. This contrasts with monolithic applications, where a single component may perform multiple tasks, leading to tight coupling and a lack of modularity.

In microservices, SRP is crucial for ensuring that services remain small, focused, and easy to manage. When each service is aligned with a specific function, it can be updated or modified independently without affecting the rest of the system.

Example of SRP in Microservices: In an e-commerce platform, instead of having one large service to handle product listings, user management, payments, and shipping, each function is broken down into individual microservices. For example:

- **User Service**: Handles user authentication and profile management.
- **Product Service**: Manages product catalogs and inventory.
- **Order Service**: Handles order processing and payments.
- **Shipping Service**: Manages shipping logistics and tracking.

By adhering to SRP, each service is easier to develop, test, deploy, and maintain. If a change is required in the shipping process, only the **Shipping Service** is updated, while other services remain unaffected.

2. Decoupling of Services

Decoupling is another key design principle in microservices architecture. Decoupling refers to the practice of separating services so that they do not depend on each other to function. Each service should operate independently, with well-defined boundaries and communication channels.

This decoupling makes the overall system more resilient and flexible. If one service fails, it does not bring down the entire application—only that specific service is impacted. Moreover, decoupled services can be developed, tested, and deployed independently by different teams, which accelerates the development process.

How Decoupling Works: In a decoupled system, services interact with each other through APIs, message brokers, or other communication protocols like HTTP or gRPC. For instance:

- **User Service** and **Order Service** communicate through REST APIs or gRPC.
- **Event-driven communication** (using message brokers like Kafka or RabbitMQ) allows services to publish and consume events asynchronously, reducing dependencies.

By decoupling services, we ensure that changes in one service don't ripple through the system, making the overall architecture more maintainable and robust.

3. Scalability in Microservices

Scalability is one of the biggest advantages of microservices architecture. In a monolithic system, scaling requires duplicating the entire application, which is inefficient and resource-heavy. In contrast, microservices allow for **horizontal scaling** of individual services.

With horizontal scaling, only the microservices that require additional resources are scaled up. For example, if the **Product Service** is under heavy load during a sale event, it can be scaled independently of the **User Service** or **Order Service**.

Types of Scaling:

- **Vertical Scaling**: Adding more resources (CPU, memory) to a single server. This works but has limitations and is less flexible for microservices.
- **Horizontal Scaling**: Adding more instances of the same microservice, distributing the load across multiple instances. This is the preferred method in microservices architecture.

Microservices can be deployed in cloud environments, which provide automatic scaling mechanisms. Cloud platforms like **Azure, AWS**, and **Google Cloud** offer services like **Kubernetes** that automatically scale microservices based on demand.

4. Fault Tolerance and Resilience

Fault tolerance is another critical design principle in microservices architecture. In distributed systems like microservices, failures are inevitable—services might crash, networks might experience delays, or databases might become temporarily unavailable. Designing microservices for fault tolerance ensures that the system remains operational even when individual components fail.

Fault Tolerance Techniques:

- **Circuit Breaker Pattern**: This pattern prevents a service from repeatedly trying to access a failed service, which could overwhelm the system. Instead, after a few failed attempts, the circuit breaker opens, preventing further calls to the failed service until it becomes available again.
- **Retry Logic**: Services can implement retry mechanisms that attempt to reconnect to a failed service after a brief pause, ensuring temporary failures don't result in permanent downtime.
- **Fallback Strategies**: When a service is unavailable, fallback strategies provide alternate responses. For example, if the **Product Service** is down, the system might display cached product information instead of showing an error message.

These techniques ensure that a microservices architecture is resilient to failure and can recover quickly from disruptions.

Setting Up Your Development Environment for .NET 8

Before you begin developing microservices, it's essential to set up your development environment. The good news is that **.NET 8** provides robust tools and libraries for building and managing microservices, and setting up the environment is straightforward.

1. Installing .NET 8 SDK and Tools

To start developing microservices using C#12 and .NET 8, you need to install the **.NET 8 SDK**. The SDK includes all the necessary libraries and tools for building, testing, and running .NET applications.

Steps to Install .NET 8 SDK:

1. **Visit the .NET 8 Website**:

- Navigate to the official .NET website to download the latest version of the .NET SDK.

1. **Choose the Correct Installer**:

- Select the appropriate installer for your operating system (Windows, macOS, or Linux).

1. **Run the Installer**:

- Follow the installation wizard to install the SDK on your machine.

1. **Verify the Installation**:

- Open a terminal or command prompt and run the following command to verify that .NET 8 has been installed correctly:

```bash
Copy code
dotnet --version
```

- This command should display the version of .NET 8 installed on your machine.

15

With .NET 8 installed, you now have access to the CLI (Command-Line Interface) for creating, building, and running .NET projects.

2. Configuring IDEs (Visual Studio, VS Code)

The choice of IDE plays a significant role in your productivity as a developer. For .NET development, **Visual Studio** and **Visual Studio Code (VS Code)** are the most popular options. Both IDEs offer excellent support for C#12, .NET 8, and microservices development.

Visual Studio

Visual Studio is Microsoft's flagship IDE for .NET development, offering a comprehensive suite of tools for building, testing, and debugging .NET applications.

Steps to Set Up Visual Studio for .NET 8:

1. **Download Visual Studio**:

- Visit the Visual Studio website and download the Community, Professional, or Enterprise edition based on your needs.

1. **Install .NET Development Workload**:

- During the installation process, select the **.NET Desktop Development** and **ASP.NET and Web Development** workloads. This will ensure that you have all the tools necessary for building microservices using .NET 8.

1. **Configure Your Environment**:

- After installation, open Visual Studio and configure your environment by creating a new **ASP.NET Core Web API** project. Visual Studio provides a project template for creating microservices.

1. **Install Extensions** (Optional):

- Visual Studio supports various extensions that enhance microservices development, such as Docker integration and Kubernetes tools. You can install these extensions from the **Visual Studio Marketplace**.

Visual Studio Code

Visual Studio Code (VS Code) is a lightweight, cross-platform code editor that is extremely popular among developers due to its versatility and extensive extension support.

Steps to Set Up VS Code for .NET 8:

1. **Download VS Code**:

- Visit the Visual Studio Code website and download the version for your operating system.

1. **Install C# Extension**:

- Once VS Code is installed, open it and navigate to the **Extensions** marketplace. Search for and install the **C# extension** by Microsoft, which provides support for .NET development, including IntelliSense, debugging, and project scaffolding.

1. **Install Docker Extension**:

- Since containerization is an integral part of microservices development, install the **Docker extension** in VS Code to manage Docker containers directly from the editor.

1. **Terminal Integration**:

- VS Code comes with built-in terminal support, making it easy to run **dotnet CLI** commands directly within the editor. This allows you to create, build, and run .NET 8 projects without switching between

17

windows.

Introduction to Docker and Containerization for Microservices

Containerization is a key technology that enables microservices to be deployed consistently across different environments. Containers provide a lightweight, portable way to package applications, along with their dependencies, into isolated units that can run on any platform. **Docker** is the most popular containerization platform, and it plays a critical role in modern microservices architecture.

What is Docker?

Docker is a tool that allows developers to package an application, along with its dependencies, into a standardized unit called a **container**. Containers are lightweight and run on any system that supports Docker, regardless of the underlying environment. This makes them ideal for microservices, as each service can be packaged into its own container and deployed independently.

Benefits of Docker in Microservices Architecture

1. **Consistency Across Environments**: Docker ensures that the application behaves the same way in development, testing, and production environments. This eliminates the "works on my machine" problem.
2. **Isolation**: Each microservice can run in its own container with its own dependencies, isolated from other services. This prevents conflicts between different versions of libraries or runtime environments.
3. **Scalability**: Docker containers can be easily scaled by running multiple instances of the same container. This makes it easy to handle increased traffic by adding more instances of specific services.
4. **Portability**: Since Docker containers can run on any system that supports Docker, microservices can be deployed to any cloud platform (Azure, AWS, Google Cloud) without modification.

Installing Docker

To use Docker in your microservices development environment, follow these steps to install Docker on your machine.

1. **Download Docker Desktop**:

- Visit the Docker website and download **Docker Desktop** for your operating system (Windows, macOS, or Linux).

1. **Install Docker**:

- Run the installer and follow the installation wizard. On Windows, Docker Desktop requires **WSL 2** (Windows Subsystem for Linux), which will be installed automatically if necessary.

1. **Verify Docker Installation**:

- After installation, open a terminal or command prompt and run the following command to verify Docker is installed correctly:

```bash
Copy code
docker --version
```

Creating Your First Docker Container

Let's walk through creating a Docker container for a simple microservice using .NET 8.

1. **Create a New .NET Project**:

- Open a terminal and create a new **ASP.NET Core Web API** project:

```bash
bash
Copy code
dotnet new webapi -n MyMicroservice
```

1. **Navigate to the Project Directory**:

```bash
bash
Copy code
cd MyMicroservice
```

1. **Create a Dockerfile**:

- A Dockerfile is a script that contains instructions for building a Docker image. Create a new file named Dockerfile in your project root and add the following content:

```dockerfile
dockerfile
Copy code
FROM mcr.microsoft.com/dotnet/aspnet:8.0 AS base
WORKDIR /app
EXPOSE 80

FROM mcr.microsoft.com/dotnet/sdk:8.0 AS build
WORKDIR /src
COPY . .
RUN dotnet restore
RUN dotnet build -c Release -o /app

FROM build AS publish
RUN dotnet publish -c Release -o /app
```

```
FROM base AS final
WORKDIR /app
COPY --from=publish /app .
ENTRYPOINT ["dotnet", "MyMicroservice.dll"]
```

1. **Build the Docker Image**:

- Run the following command to build the Docker image:

```
bash
Copy code
docker build -t mymicroservice .
```

1. **Run the Docker Container**:

- Once the image is built, you can run it as a container:

```
bash
Copy code
docker run -d -p 8080:80 mymicroservice
```

1. **Access the Microservice**:

- Open your web browser and navigate to http://localhost:8080. You should see the default response from your microservice.

By using Docker, you can package and deploy your microservices efficiently, ensuring consistency across environments and making it easy to scale and manage individual services.

Conclusion

In this chapter, we covered the foundational principles of microservices architecture, including **Single Responsibility**, **Decoupling**, **Scalability**, and **Fault Tolerance**. We also walked through setting up your development environment, including installing .NET 8 and configuring popular IDEs like Visual Studio and VS Code. Finally, we introduced **Docker** and containerization, demonstrating how to package and deploy a microservice in a Docker container.

With this groundwork laid, you're ready to dive deeper into microservices architecture and begin building scalable, resilient applications using **C#12** and **.NET 8**. In the following chapters, we'll explore more advanced topics such as inter-service communication, design patterns, security, and cloud deployment.

Chapter 2: Building Your First Microservice with C#12 and .NET 8

Microservices have gained widespread popularity in the development community for enabling modularity, scalability, and flexibility. In this chapter, we will take a deep dive into the practicalities of **building your first microservice** using **C#12** and **.NET 8**. Starting from scratch, we will walk through project creation, explore minimal APIs, implement service-to-service communication using REST and gRPC, and finally demonstrate how to test the microservice locally before deployment.

By the end of this chapter, you will have a fully functioning microservice built with the latest technologies available in .NET 8, leveraging modern C#12 features that simplify code development and management. You will also understand how to structure, design, and expose APIs from your microservice.

Section 1: Creating a Microservice Project with .NET 8

Before diving into coding, we need to create the foundational structure for our microservice. In this section, you will learn how to set up a new project specifically designed for microservices development, utilizing the project scaffolding tools available in .NET 8.

Step 1: Project Initialization with .NET CLI

To begin with, we will use the **dotnet CLI** (Command-Line Interface) to generate a new ASP.NET Core Web API project that will serve as the skeleton for our microservice. Open your terminal and navigate to the directory where you'd like to create your project. Run the following command:

```bash
Copy code
dotnet new webapi -n ProductService
```

This command generates a new Web API project named **ProductService**, which could represent the microservice responsible for managing product data in an e-commerce application.

After the command completes, navigate into the project directory:

```bash
Copy code
cd ProductService
```

Step 2: Understanding the Generated Structure

The generated structure includes various files and directories:

- **Controllers**: Contains API controllers, which handle HTTP requests.
- **Program.cs**: The entry point for the application where services are configured and middleware is set up.
- **appsettings.json**: Contains application configuration settings, like database connection strings.
- **Properties/launchSettings.json**: Holds settings for launching the application in different environments (e.g., development, production).

This structure is typical for ASP.NET Core applications, but in microservices, you will generally keep the services small and focused. For our purposes, we will concentrate on a single controller responsible for managing product data.

Section 2: Minimal APIs in .NET 8

One of the most exciting features in .NET 8 is the introduction of **minimal APIs**. Minimal APIs allow you to build lightweight microservices quickly with minimal boilerplate code. Instead of using the traditional controller-based approach, minimal APIs allow developers to define endpoints directly in the Program.cs file.

Step 1: Setting Up Minimal APIs in Program.cs

Let's update our Program.cs file to implement a minimal API. Start by removing the default code and replacing it with the following:

```csharp
Copy code
var builder = WebApplication.CreateBuilder(args);
var app = builder.Build();

app.MapGet("/api/products", () => new List<Product>
{
    new Product { Id = 1, Name = "Laptop", Price = 1200 },
    new Product { Id = 2, Name = "Smartphone", Price = 800 }
});

app.Run();

public class Product
{
    public int Id { get; set; }
    public string Name { get; set; }
    public double Price { get; set; }
}
```

In this minimal API, we define a single endpoint that returns a list of products. This API responds to GET requests on the /api/products route.

Here's a breakdown of the code:

- **MapGet**: This method maps an HTTP GET request to a specific route. It takes two arguments: the route and the response. In our case, it returns a list of Product objects.
- **Product Class**: This class defines the data structure for products, with properties for Id, Name, and Price.

Run the project using:

```bash
Copy code
dotnet run
```

Navigate to http://localhost:5000/api/products, and you should see a JSON response with product data.

Step 2: Adding More API Endpoints

Now, let's extend our minimal API to include more functionality like creating, updating, and deleting products. Update the Program.cs file with the following code:

```csharp
Copy code
var builder = WebApplication.CreateBuilder(args);
var app = builder.Build();

var products = new List<Product>
{
    new Product { Id = 1, Name = "Laptop", Price = 1200 },
    new Product { Id = 2, Name = "Smartphone", Price = 800 }
};

app.MapGet("/api/products", () => products);

app.MapGet("/api/products/{id}", (int id) =>
{
    var product = products.FirstOrDefault(p => p.Id == id);
```

```
    return product != null ? Results.Ok(product) :
    Results.NotFound();
});

app.MapPost("/api/products", (Product product) =>
{
    product.Id = products.Max(p => p.Id) + 1;
    products.Add(product);
    return Results.Created($"/api/products/{product.Id}",
    product);
});

app.MapPut("/api/products/{id}", (int id, Product updatedProduct)
=>
{
    var product = products.FirstOrDefault(p => p.Id == id);
    if (product is null) return Results.NotFound();

    product.Name = updatedProduct.Name;
    product.Price = updatedProduct.Price;
    return Results.NoContent();
});

app.MapDelete("/api/products/{id}", (int id) =>
{
    var product = products.FirstOrDefault(p => p.Id == id);
    if (product is null) return Results.NotFound();

    products.Remove(product);
    return Results.NoContent();
});

app.Run();

public class Product
{
    public int Id { get; set; }
    public string Name { get; set; }
    public double Price { get; set; }
}
```

Here, we added four additional endpoints:

- **Get by Id**: Returns a specific product by its Id.
- **Create Product**: Adds a new product to the list.
- **Update Product**: Updates an existing product.
- **Delete Product**: Deletes a product by its Id.

Each API method uses standard HTTP verbs (GET, POST, PUT, DELETE) and HTTP status codes like OK, Created, NotFound, and NoContent.

This minimal API approach simplifies the code and makes it easier to manage small microservices without the need for the traditional controller structure.

Section 3: Service Communication Patterns

Microservices need to communicate with each other, and the choice of communication protocol plays a crucial role in the design of a microservice architecture. In this section, we will explore the two most common communication mechanisms: **REST** and **gRPC**.

RESTful Communication

REST (Representational State Transfer) is the most commonly used communication protocol for microservices. REST relies on standard HTTP methods (GET, POST, PUT, DELETE) and URLs to interact with different services.

In the example we've built so far, our microservice exposes a RESTful API for managing products. RESTful APIs are easy to consume and widely supported across different programming languages, making them ideal for communication between microservices.

Example Use Case: Imagine that in our e-commerce system, we have a **ProductService** and an **OrderService**. The **OrderService** might need to fetch product information by calling the RESTful API exposed by the **ProductService**.

To make this API request, the **OrderService** can send a GET request to

/api/products/{id} to fetch product details before processing an order.

gRPC Communication

gRPC is a high-performance, open-source framework that enables communication between services using HTTP/2. It provides a more efficient binary protocol compared to REST's text-based JSON payloads. This makes gRPC especially useful in scenarios where performance and low latency are critical.

Let's modify our **ProductService** to expose a **gRPC** endpoint.

Step 1: Adding gRPC Support

To add gRPC support, first modify the ProductService.csproj file to include gRPC:

```xml
Copy code
<Project Sdk="Microsoft.NET.Sdk.Web">

  <PropertyGroup>
    <TargetFramework>net8.0</TargetFramework>
  </PropertyGroup>

  <ItemGroup>
    <PackageReference Include="Grpc.AspNetCore" Version="2.39.0"
    />
  </ItemGroup>

</Project>
```

Next, create a new folder named **Protos** and add a **product.proto** file. The .proto file defines the contract for gRPC services.

product.proto:

```protobuf
Copy code
syntax = "proto3";

option csharp_namespace = "ProductService";
```

```
service Product {
  rpc GetProductById(ProductRequest) returns (ProductReply);
}

message ProductRequest {
  int32 id = 1;
}

message ProductReply {
  int32 id = 1;
  string name = 2;
  double price = 3;
}
```

The .proto file defines a GetProductById RPC method that takes a ProductRequest and returns a ProductReply.

Step 2: Implementing gRPC in Program.cs

Now update the Program.cs to add support for gRPC:

```csharp
Copy code
var builder = WebApplication.CreateBuilder(args);
builder.Services.AddGrpc();

var app = builder.Build();

app.MapGrpcService<ProductService>();

app.MapGet("/", () => "gRPC server is running.");

app.Run();
```

Next, create a new class called **ProductService.cs** to implement the gRPC service:

```csharp
Copy code
public class ProductService : Product.ProductBase
{
    private readonly List<Product> products = new List<Product>
    {
        new Product { Id = 1, Name = "Laptop", Price = 1200 },
        new Product { Id = 2, Name = "Smartphone", Price = 800 }
    };

    public override Task<ProductReply>
    GetProductById(ProductRequest request, ServerCallContext
    context)
    {
        var product = products.FirstOrDefault(p => p.Id ==
        request.Id);
        if (product == null) return Task.FromResult(new
        ProductReply());

        return Task.FromResult(new ProductReply
        {
            Id = product.Id,
            Name = product.Name,
            Price = product.Price
        });
    }
}

public class Product
{
    public int Id { get; set; }
    public string Name { get; set; }
    public double Price { get; set; }
}
```

In this implementation:

- The ProductService class inherits from the base class generated by the .proto file (Product.ProductBase).

- The GetProductById method processes the incoming gRPC request and returns a ProductReply.

Now, your microservice can communicate using both REST and gRPC, offering flexibility for different consumers of the service.

Section 4: Testing the Microservice Locally

Once your microservice is built, you need to test it to ensure it works as expected. Let's explore testing methods, including unit tests and integration tests.

Unit Testing

Unit testing is critical in microservices because each service is isolated, and you want to verify the logic of individual components. Let's create a unit test for the ProductService.

1. **Create a Test Project**: Run the following command to create a new test project:

```bash
Copy code
dotnet new xunit -n ProductService.Tests
```

1. **Write Unit Tests**: In the ProductService.Tests project, create a test for the ProductService class:

```csharp
Copy code
public class ProductServiceTests
{
```

```
[Fact]
public void GetProductById_ReturnsProduct_WhenProductExists()
{
    // Arrange
    var service = new ProductService();
    var request = new ProductRequest { Id = 1 };

    // Act
    var result = service.GetProductById(request, null).Result;

    // Assert
    Assert.Equal(1, result.Id);
    Assert.Equal("Laptop", result.Name);
    Assert.Equal(1200, result.Price);
}

[Fact]
public void
GetProductById_ReturnsEmpty_WhenProductDoesNotExist()
{
    // Arrange
    var service = new ProductService();
    var request = new ProductRequest { Id = 999 };

    // Act
    var result = service.GetProductById(request, null).Result;

    // Assert
    Assert.Equal(0, result.Id);
    Assert.Null(result.Name);
    Assert.Equal(0, result.Price);
}
}
```

Run the tests using:

```bash
Copy code
```

33

```
dotnet test
```

The test project ensures that the microservice's business logic works as expected.

Integration Testing

Integration testing verifies that the microservice works when it interacts with external systems or other services.

To set up integration tests, you can use tools like **Postman** to manually test REST and gRPC APIs or use automated testing tools like **k6** for load testing.

Conclusion

In this chapter, we've covered the process of building your first microservice using C#12 and .NET 8. You learned how to:

- Set up a microservice project.
- Use minimal APIs to build lightweight services.
- Implement both REST and gRPC communication for flexibility.
- Write unit and integration tests to ensure the reliability of your microservice.

Armed with this knowledge, you are ready to expand on this foundation by exploring more advanced topics like deploying microservices to the cloud, implementing security, and scaling services—topics we will cover in the upcoming chapters.

Chapter 3: Microservices Design Patterns

Microservices architecture allows organizations to create applications that are more flexible, scalable, and maintainable. However, simply splitting an application into microservices isn't enough to guarantee these benefits. To build resilient and efficient systems, developers must use **design patterns** that solve common challenges encountered in distributed systems. These patterns provide standardized solutions to address inter-service communication, fault tolerance, scalability, data management, and transaction handling.

In this chapter, we will explore essential design patterns for microservices architecture and how to implement them using **C#12** and **.NET 8**. We'll cover patterns like the **API Gateway**, **Service Discovery**, **Circuit Breaker**, **Saga**, and **CQRS**. By the end of this chapter, you will understand how to apply these patterns to real-world scenarios, ensuring that your microservices are robust, scalable, and resilient to failure.

Section 1: API Gateway Pattern

The **API Gateway** pattern is one of the most commonly used design patterns in microservices architecture. It serves as a single entry point for clients to interact with multiple backend services. Without an API gateway, clients would need to interact directly with each microservice, which increases complexity and creates challenges in terms of security, load balancing, and service discovery.

1.1 Overview of the API Gateway Pattern

In the **API Gateway** pattern, the gateway acts as a reverse proxy that routes client requests to the appropriate microservices. It can also handle additional responsibilities such as:

- **Authentication**: Validating client requests before forwarding them to backend services.
- **Rate Limiting**: Limiting the number of requests from clients to prevent abuse or overloading of services.
- **Request Aggregation**: Aggregating responses from multiple microservices and returning a single response to the client.
- **Caching**: Caching responses from microservices to improve performance and reduce the load on backend services.

By centralizing these cross-cutting concerns in the API Gateway, you can simplify the design of individual microservices and reduce the complexity of managing client interactions.

1.2 Implementing an API Gateway in .NET 8

To implement an API Gateway in .NET 8, you can use the **YARP (Yet Another Reverse Proxy)** library, which provides reverse proxy capabilities with minimal configuration. Let's walk through creating a basic API Gateway using YARP.

Step 1: Installing YARP in Your API Gateway Project

Start by creating a new ASP.NET Core project for the API Gateway:

```bash
Copy code
dotnet new web -n APIGateway
cd APIGateway
```

Next, install the YARP package via the **dotnet CLI**:

```bash
bash
Copy code
dotnet add package Yarp.ReverseProxy
```

Step 2: Configuring the API Gateway

In the Program.cs file, configure YARP to route requests to backend microservices:

```csharp
csharp
Copy code
var builder = WebApplication.CreateBuilder(args);

builder.Services.AddReverseProxy()
    .LoadFromConfig(builder.Configuration.GetSection("ReverseProxy"));

var app = builder.Build();

app.MapReverseProxy();

app.Run();
```

Next, modify the appsettings.json file to define routing rules for backend services:

```json
json
Copy code
{
  "ReverseProxy": {
    "Routes": [
      {
        "RouteId": "productRoute",
        "ClusterId": "productCluster",
        "Match": {
          "Path": "/api/products/{**catch-all}"
        }
      },
      {
```

37

```
      "RouteId": "orderRoute",
      "ClusterId": "orderCluster",
      "Match": {
        "Path": "/api/orders/{**catch-all}"
      }
    }
  ],
  "Clusters": {
    "productCluster": {
      "Destinations": {
        "productService": {
          "Address": "http://localhost:5001/"
        }
      }
    },
    "orderCluster": {
      "Destinations": {
        "orderService": {
          "Address": "http://localhost:5002/"
        }
      }
    }
  }
}
```

In this configuration:

- Requests to /api/products are routed to the **ProductService** running on localhost:5001.
- Requests to /api/orders are routed to the **OrderService** running on localhost:5002.

Step 3: Running the API Gateway

Run the API Gateway project using:

```bash
Copy code
dotnet run
```

With this setup, the API Gateway will now route incoming requests to the appropriate microservices, simplifying client interactions with your backend services. Additional features like rate limiting, caching, and authentication can be implemented in the gateway to further enhance your system.

Section 2: Service Discovery Pattern

In a microservices architecture, services often run on dynamic environments like containers or cloud platforms where the IP addresses and locations of services can change frequently. **Service Discovery** helps microservices find and communicate with each other without hardcoding addresses.

2.1 Types of Service Discovery

There are two primary types of service discovery:

- **Client-Side Discovery**: The client is responsible for determining the location of a service by querying a service registry (e.g., **Consul**, **Eureka**). Once the client retrieves the address of a service, it can communicate directly with it.
- **Server-Side Discovery**: The client sends requests to a load balancer (or API Gateway), which queries the service registry and routes the request to the correct instance.

2.2 Implementing Server-Side Discovery with Consul

Let's implement **Server-Side Discovery** using **Consul**, a popular service registry tool. Consul allows microservices to register their availability and health with a central registry, enabling other services (or the API Gateway) to discover them dynamically.

Step 1: Installing Consul

Start by installing Consul on your machine. You can download it from the official Consul website.

Once installed, run Consul in development mode:

```bash
Copy code
consul agent -dev
```

Step 2: Configuring Microservices to Register with Consul

Let's modify our **ProductService** to register itself with Consul. First, install the Consul NuGet package:

```bash
Copy code
dotnet add package Consul
```

Next, update the Program.cs file to register the service with Consul:

```csharp
Copy code
var builder = WebApplication.CreateBuilder(args);

builder.Services.AddControllers();
builder.Services.AddSingleton<IConsulClient, ConsulClient>(c =>
new ConsulClient(config =>
{
    config.Address = new Uri("http://localhost:8500");
}));

var app = builder.Build();

app.UseRouting();
app.UseEndpoints(endpoints => { endpoints.MapControllers(); });

var lifetime = app.Lifetime;
var consulClient =
app.Services.GetRequiredService<IConsulClient>();
```

```
var registration = new AgentServiceRegistration
{
    ID = "product-service",
    Name = "ProductService",
    Address = "localhost",
    Port = 5001,
    Check = new AgentServiceCheck
    {
        HTTP = "http://localhost:5001/health",
        Interval = TimeSpan.FromSeconds(10)
    }
};

await consulClient.Agent.ServiceRegister(registration,
CancellationToken.None);

lifetime.ApplicationStopping.Register(async () =>
{
    await consulClient.Agent.ServiceDeregister("product-service",
    CancellationToken.None);
});

app.Run();
```

This code registers the **ProductService** with Consul at startup and deregisters it when the service shuts down. The health check ensures that Consul knows the service is running correctly.

Step 3: Discovering Services in the API Gateway

Finally, update the **API Gateway** to use Consul for discovering the **ProductService** dynamically:

```
csharp
Copy code
builder.Services.AddSingleton<IConsulClient, ConsulClient>(c =>
new ConsulClient(config =>
{
```

```
    config.Address = new Uri("http://localhost:8500");
}));

builder.Services.AddReverseProxy()
    .LoadFromMemory(GetRoutesFromConsul());

app.MapReverseProxy();

static IEnumerable<RouteConfig> GetRoutesFromConsul()
{
    var consulClient = new ConsulClient(c => c.Address = new
    Uri("http://localhost:8500"));
    var services = consulClient.Agent.Services().Result.Response;

    foreach (var service in services)
    {
        yield return new RouteConfig
        {
            RouteId = service.Value.Service,
            ClusterId = service.Value.Service,
            Match = new RouteMatch { Path =
            $"/{service.Value.Service}/{{**catch-all}}" },
            Transforms = new List<IDictionary<string, string>> {
            new Dictionary<string, string> { ["PathRemovePrefix"]
            = $"/{service.Value.Service}" } }
        };
    }
}
```

With this configuration, the **API Gateway** now queries Consul to discover available services dynamically. As new services are registered or existing services are removed, the API Gateway adjusts its routing rules automatically.

Section 3: Circuit Breaker Pattern

In distributed systems like microservices, services often depend on other services, and failures in one service can propagate throughout the system. The **Circuit Breaker** pattern is designed to prevent cascading failures by stopping repeated attempts to call a service that is failing or under heavy load.

3.1 How the Circuit Breaker Works

The Circuit Breaker pattern monitors the number of failures in a service and determines when to "trip" the breaker. Once tripped, the circuit breaker short-circuits requests and returns an error immediately, preventing the system from being overwhelmed. After a timeout period, the breaker switches to a "half-open" state, allowing a limited number of requests through to see if the service has recovered.

3.2 Implementing Circuit Breaker in .NET 8 with Polly

Polly is a popular resilience and transient-fault-handling library for .NET that provides an easy way to implement the Circuit Breaker pattern. Let's walk through adding Polly to a microservice to implement circuit breaking.

Step 1: Installing Polly

Start by installing the **Polly** NuGet package in your project:

```bash
Copy code
dotnet add package Polly
```

Step 2: Implementing Circuit Breaker in HTTP Calls

Suppose our **OrderService** needs to communicate with the **Product-Service** to retrieve product details. We'll wrap the HTTP calls to the **ProductService** with a Polly Circuit Breaker.

```csharp
Copy code
var circuitBreakerPolicy = Policy
    .Handle<HttpRequestException>()
    .CircuitBreakerAsync(2, TimeSpan.FromSeconds(30));

var productServiceUrl = "http://localhost:5001/api/products";

try
```

```
{
    await circuitBreakerPolicy.ExecuteAsync(async () =>
    {
        var response = await
        httpClient.GetAsync($"{productServiceUrl}/{productId}");
        response.EnsureSuccessStatusCode();

        var product = await
        response.Content.ReadAsAsync<Product>();
        Console.WriteLine($"Product Name: {product.Name}");
    });
}
catch (BrokenCircuitException)
{
    Console.WriteLine("ProductService is currently unavailable.");
}
```

In this example:

- The Circuit Breaker will trip after 2 consecutive failed HTTP requests.
- Once tripped, the breaker will remain open for 30 seconds, during which any requests to the **ProductService** will be short-circuited.
- After 30 seconds, the Circuit Breaker will enter a half-open state and allow a limited number of requests to pass through to check if the service has recovered.

Using Polly, you can easily integrate the Circuit Breaker pattern to prevent cascading failures in your microservices architecture.

Section 4: Saga Pattern

The **Saga** pattern is essential for managing long-running transactions in a microservices architecture. Unlike monolithic systems, where transactions can be handled easily with a single database, microservices often involve multiple distributed services with independent databases. The Saga pattern coordinates these distributed transactions by breaking them down into a

44

series of local transactions, each of which can be compensated if something goes wrong.

4.1 Types of Sagas

There are two primary types of Sagas:

- **Choreography**: Each service involved in the saga performs a local transaction and then publishes an event or message to notify the next service.
- **Orchestration**: A centralized orchestrator coordinates the saga by calling each service in sequence and handling rollback if necessary.

4.2 Implementing Choreography-Based Saga with RabbitMQ

Let's implement a **Choreography-based Saga** using **RabbitMQ** to manage distributed transactions. In our scenario, the **OrderService** and **PaymentService** will participate in the saga to process an order.

Step 1: Installing RabbitMQ and Setting Up Messaging

Install RabbitMQ on your system and run it. You can use Docker to run RabbitMQ quickly:

```bash
Copy code
docker run -d --hostname my-rabbit --name rabbitmq -p 5672:5672
-p 15672:15672 rabbitmq:3-management
```

Install the RabbitMQ.Client NuGet package in your **OrderService** and **PaymentService** projects:

```bash
Copy code
dotnet add package RabbitMQ.Client
```

Step 2: Implementing the Saga in the OrderService

In the **OrderService**, after an order is placed, publish an event to RabbitMQ to notify the **PaymentService**:

```csharp
Copy code
var factory = new ConnectionFactory { HostName = "localhost" };
using var connection = factory.CreateConnection();
using var channel = connection.CreateModel();

channel.QueueDeclare(queue: "orderQueue", durable: false,
exclusive: false, autoDelete: false, arguments: null);

var order = new { OrderId = 123, Amount = 150.00 };

var body =
Encoding.UTF8.GetBytes(JsonConvert.SerializeObject(order));

channel.BasicPublish(exchange: "", routingKey: "orderQueue",
basicProperties: null, body: body);

Console.WriteLine("Order placed: {0}", order.OrderId);
```

Step 3: Processing the Event in PaymentService

In the **PaymentService**, subscribe to the **orderQueue** and process payments:

```csharp
Copy code
var factory = new ConnectionFactory { HostName = "localhost" };
using var connection = factory.CreateConnection();
using var channel = connection.CreateModel();

channel.QueueDeclare(queue: "orderQueue", durable: false,
exclusive: false, autoDelete: false, arguments: null);

var consumer = new EventingBasicConsumer(channel);
consumer.Received += (model, ea) =>
{
    var body = ea.Body.ToArray();
    var message = Encoding.UTF8.GetString(body);
```

```
    var order = JsonConvert.DeserializeObject<Order>(message);

    Console.WriteLine("Processing payment for Order: {0}",
    order.OrderId);
    // Perform payment processing logic here
};

channel.BasicConsume(queue: "orderQueue", autoAck: true,
consumer: consumer);

Console.WriteLine("Waiting for orders...");
Console.ReadLine();
```

This setup demonstrates how to implement a Saga using the **Choreography** model, where each service performs its local transaction and notifies the next service using events.

Section 5: CQRS Pattern

The **CQRS (Command Query Responsibility Segregation)** pattern is used to separate **write** and **read** operations in a system. In microservices, this pattern helps optimize performance by allowing queries to be handled separately from commands, which may involve more complex business logic.

5.1 Overview of CQRS

In traditional systems, the same model is used for both reading and writing data, which can lead to performance bottlenecks, especially in systems with a high volume of reads. The CQRS pattern solves this problem by using different models for handling reads (queries) and writes (commands). This separation allows you to optimize each operation independently.

- **Command**: Handles the business logic to change data. For example, creating or updating a product in the **ProductService**.
- **Query**: Handles the retrieval of data without modifying it. For example, fetching product details in the **ProductService**.

47

5.2 Implementing CQRS in the ProductService

Let's implement the **CQRS** pattern in the **ProductService**. We will create separate command and query handlers for managing products.

Step 1: Creating the Command Handlers

First, create a **CommandHandler** to handle write operations like adding or updating a product:

```csharp
Copy code
public class ProductCommandHandler
{
    private readonly List<Product> _products = new
    List<Product>();

    public Product AddProduct(string name, double price)
    {
        var product = new Product { Id = _products.Count + 1,
        Name = name, Price = price };
        _products.Add(product);
        return product;
    }

    public void UpdateProduct(int id, string name, double price)
    {
        var product = _products.FirstOrDefault(p => p.Id == id);
        if (product != null)
        {
            product.Name = name;
            product.Price = price;
        }
    }
}
```

Step 2: Creating the Query Handlers

Next, create a **QueryHandler** to handle read operations like fetching product details:

```csharp
Copy code
public class ProductQueryHandler
{
    private readonly List<Product> _products = new List<Product>
    {
        new Product { Id = 1, Name = "Laptop", Price = 1200 },
        new Product { Id = 2, Name = "Smartphone", Price = 800 }
    };

    public Product GetProductById(int id)
    {
        return _products.FirstOrDefault(p => p.Id == id);
    }

    public IEnumerable<Product> GetAllProducts()
    {
        return _products;
    }
}
```

Step 3: Wiring Up CQRS in the API

Finally, modify the API to use the command and query handlers:

```csharp
Copy code
var builder = WebApplication.CreateBuilder(args);

builder.Services.AddSingleton<ProductCommandHandler>();
builder.Services.AddSingleton<ProductQueryHandler>();

var app = builder.Build();

app.MapGet("/api/products", (ProductQueryHandler queryHandler) =>
queryHandler.GetAllProducts());
app.MapGet("/api/products/{id}", (int id, ProductQueryHandler
queryHandler) => queryHandler.GetProductById(id));
app.MapPost("/api/products", (string name, double price,
ProductCommandHandler commandHandler) =>
```

```
{
    var product = commandHandler.AddProduct(name, price);
    return Results.Created($"/api/products/{product.Id}",
    product);
});

app.Run();
```

This implementation separates the read and write concerns, ensuring that each operation can be optimized independently.

Conclusion

In this chapter, we explored essential design patterns for microservices architecture, including:

- The **API Gateway** pattern for routing and handling client requests.
- **Service Discovery** for dynamically locating microservices.
- The **Circuit Breaker** pattern for fault tolerance and resilience.
- The **Saga** pattern for managing distributed transactions.
- The **CQRS**

pattern for separating read and write operations.

By implementing these patterns using **C#12** and **.NET 8**, you can build robust, scalable, and maintainable microservices that meet modern application requirements. In the next chapter, we will delve into inter-service communication mechanisms, security practices, and additional strategies for ensuring the resilience and performance of your microservices architecture.

Chapter 4: Inter-Service Communication in Microservices

In a microservices architecture, effective communication between services is crucial for ensuring smooth operation and overall system functionality. Unlike monolithic applications where all components reside in a single codebase, microservices must interact over the network, which introduces new complexities. This chapter delves into the various communication mechanisms available in microservices, their respective advantages and disadvantages, and how to implement them using C#12 and .NET 8.

We will explore **RESTful APIs**, **gRPC**, **message brokers**, and **event-driven architectures**, as well as best practices for ensuring robust and efficient communication. By the end of this chapter, you will understand the trade-offs of different communication styles and how to implement them effectively in your microservices.

Section 1: RESTful APIs

REST (Representational State Transfer) is one of the most widely used communication protocols in microservices architecture. RESTful APIs provide a simple, stateless way for services to communicate over HTTP.

1.1 Overview of RESTful APIs

RESTful APIs leverage standard HTTP methods (GET, POST, PUT, DELETE) to perform CRUD (Create, Read, Update, Delete) operations. The key characteristics of RESTful APIs include:

- **Statelessness**: Each request from a client to a server must contain all the information needed to understand and process the request. The server does not store any session information about the client.
- **Resource-Based**: Resources are identified using URIs (Uniform Resource Identifiers). Each resource can be manipulated using standard HTTP methods.
- **Use of Standard HTTP Status Codes**: REST APIs utilize standard HTTP status codes to indicate the outcome of API calls (e.g., 200 OK, 404 Not Found, 500 Internal Server Error).

1.2 Implementing a RESTful API with .NET 8

Let's build on the previous chapters and implement a RESTful API for managing products in our **ProductService**.

Step 1: Setting Up the ProductService

If you haven't already, create a new ASP.NET Core Web API project for the **ProductService**:

```bash
Copy code
dotnet new webapi -n ProductService
cd ProductService
```

Step 2: Defining the Product Model

Create a Product class in the Models folder:

```csharp
Copy code
namespace ProductService.Models
{
    public class Product
```

```csharp
    {
        public int Id { get; set; }
        public string Name { get; set; }
        public double Price { get; set; }
    }
}
```

Step 3: Creating the Product Controller

Create a controller called ProductController in the Controllers folder to handle API requests:

```csharp
csharp
Copy code
using Microsoft.AspNetCore.Mvc;
using ProductService.Models;
using System.Collections.Generic;
using System.Linq;

namespace ProductService.Controllers
{
    [ApiController]
    [Route("api/products")]
    public class ProductController : ControllerBase
    {
        private static List<Product> products = new List<Product>
        {
            new Product { Id = 1, Name = "Laptop", Price = 1200 },
            new Product { Id = 2, Name = "Smartphone", Price =
            800 }
        };

        [HttpGet]
        public ActionResult<IEnumerable<Product>> GetProducts()
        {
            return Ok(products);
        }

        [HttpGet("{id}")]
        public ActionResult<Product> GetProduct(int id)
```

```
{
    var product = products.FirstOrDefault(p => p.Id ==
    id);
    if (product == null)
        return NotFound();

    return Ok(product);
}

[HttpPost]
public ActionResult<Product> CreateProduct(Product
product)
{
    product.Id = products.Max(p => p.Id) + 1;
    products.Add(product);
    return CreatedAtAction(nameof(GetProduct), new {, id =
    product.Id }, product);
}

[HttpPut("{id}")]
public IActionResult UpdateProduct(int id, Product
updatedProduct)
{
    var product = products.FirstOrDefault(p => p.Id ==
    id);
    if (product == null)
        return NotFound();

    product.Name = updatedProduct.Name;
    product.Price = updatedProduct.Price;

    return NoContent();
}

[HttpDelete("{id}")]
public IActionResult DeleteProduct(int id)
{
    var product = products.FirstOrDefault(p => p.Id ==
    id);
    if (product == null)
```

```
        return NotFound();

    products.Remove(product);
    return NoContent();
    }
  }
}
```

In this controller:

- **GetProducts**: Returns all products.
- **GetProduct**: Retrieves a product by ID.
- **CreateProduct**: Adds a new product.
- **UpdateProduct**: Updates an existing product.
- **DeleteProduct**: Removes a product by ID.

Step 4: Testing the RESTful API
  Run the **ProductService**:

```bash
Copy code
dotnet run
```

You can test the API endpoints using **Postman** or **cURL**.
  For example, to retrieve all products, send a GET request to:

```bash
Copy code
http://localhost:5000/api/products
```

To create a new product, send a POST request with a JSON body:

55

```json
Copy code
{
    "name": "Tablet",
    "price": 600
}
```

You will see how easy it is to manage products using a RESTful API.

Section 2: gRPC Communication

gRPC (gRPC Remote Procedure Calls) is another popular communication protocol for microservices, particularly suited for high-performance applications. It is based on HTTP/2 and uses Protocol Buffers as the interface description language.

2.1 Advantages of gRPC

- **High Performance**: gRPC uses binary serialization (Protocol Buffers), making it faster and more efficient than JSON used in REST.
- **Bidirectional Streaming**: gRPC supports bidirectional streaming, allowing clients and servers to send messages in both directions.
- **Strongly Typed Contracts**: gRPC uses Protocol Buffers to define service contracts, ensuring type safety and reducing serialization issues.

2.2 Implementing a gRPC Service with .NET 8

Let's implement a gRPC service to manage products alongside the REST API we created.

Step 1: Adding gRPC Support

Ensure you have the Grpc.AspNetCore package installed:

```bash
Copy code
dotnet add package Grpc.AspNetCore
```

Step 2: Creating the gRPC Service Definition

Create a folder named **Protos** and add a new file called product.proto. Define your gRPC service:

```protobuf
Copy code
syntax = "proto3";

option csharp_namespace = "ProductService.Protos";

service Product {
    rpc GetProductById(ProductRequest) returns (ProductReply);
    rpc CreateProduct(ProductRequest) returns (ProductReply);
    rpc UpdateProduct(ProductUpdateRequest) returns
    (ProductReply);
    rpc DeleteProduct(ProductRequest) returns (ProductReply);
}

message ProductRequest {
    int32 id = 1;
}

message ProductReply {
    int32 id = 1;
    string name = 2;
    double price = 3;
}

message ProductUpdateRequest {
    int32 id = 1;
    string name = 2;
    double price = 3;
}
```

Step 3: Implementing the gRPC Service

Create a new class called ProductService that implements the generated base class from the .proto file:

```csharp
Copy code
using Grpc.Core;
using ProductService.Models;
using System.Collections.Generic;
using System.Linq;
using System.Threading.Tasks;

namespace ProductService
{
    public class ProductService : Protos.Product.ProductBase
    {
        private readonly List<Product> _products = new
        List<Product>
        {
            new Product { Id = 1, Name = "Laptop", Price = 1200 },
            new Product { Id = 2, Name = "Smartphone", Price =
            800 }
        };

        public override Task<ProductReply>
        GetProductById(ProductRequest request, ServerCallContext
        context)
        {
            var product = _products.FirstOrDefault(p => p.Id ==
            request.Id);
            return Task.FromResult(new ProductReply
            {
                Id = product?.Id ?? 0,
                Name = product?.Name ?? "",
                Price = product?.Price ?? 0
            });
        }

        public override Task<ProductReply>
        CreateProduct(ProductRequest request, ServerCallContext
        context)
        {
            var product = new Product { Id = _products.Count + 1,
            Name = request.Name, Price = request.Price };
```

```
    _products.Add(product);
    return Task.FromResult(new ProductReply { Id =
    product.Id, Name = product.Name, Price =
    product.Price });
}

public override Task<ProductReply>
UpdateProduct(ProductUpdateRequest request,
ServerCallContext context)
{
    var product = _products.FirstOrDefault(p => p.Id ==
    request.Id);
    if (product != null)
    {
        product.Name = request.Name;
        product.Price = request.Price;
    }
    return Task.FromResult(new ProductReply { Id =
    product?.Id ?? 0 });
}

public override Task<ProductReply>
DeleteProduct(ProductRequest request, ServerCallContext
context)
{
    var product = _products.FirstOrDefault(p => p.Id ==
    request.Id);
    if (product != null)
    {
        _products.Remove(product);
    }
    return Task.FromResult(new ProductReply { Id =
    product?.Id ?? 0 });
}
    }
}
```

Step 4: Configuring gRPC in Program.cs

Update the Program.cs to register the gRPC service:

```csharp
Copy code
var builder = WebApplication.CreateBuilder(args);

builder.Services.AddGrpc();

var app = builder.Build();

app.MapGrpcService<ProductService>();
app.MapGet("/", () => "gRPC server is running.");

app.Run();
```

Step 5: Testing the gRPC Service

You can use **gRPC clients** like **gRPCurl** or create a simple console application to test the gRPC service.

For example, to test GetProductById, use the following gRPCurl command:

```bash
Copy code
grpcurl -plaintext localhost:5000
ProductService.Product/GetProductById -d '{"id": 1}'
```

You should receive a response containing the product details.

Section 3: Message Brokers and Event-Driven Architecture

In microservices, it's essential to decouple services to achieve flexibility and maintainability. One effective way to achieve this is by using **message brokers** and implementing an **event-driven architecture**.

3.1 Overview of Message Brokers

A **message broker** is an intermediary that allows services to communicate with each other by sending messages asynchronously. Instead of making direct calls between services, microservices can publish messages to a message broker, which then routes the messages to the appropriate services.

Common message brokers include:

- **RabbitMQ**
- **Apache Kafka**
- **Azure Service Bus**
- **AWS SQS**

Message brokers provide several benefits:

- **Decoupling**: Services are decoupled from one another, allowing for greater flexibility in development and deployment.
- **Asynchronous Communication**: Services can send messages without waiting for a response, improving performance and responsiveness.
- **Reliability**: Message brokers often provide persistence and delivery guarantees, ensuring messages are not lost during transmission.

3.2 Implementing Event-Driven Architecture with RabbitMQ

Let's implement an event-driven architecture using RabbitMQ in our microservices system. We will set up a **ProductService** that publishes product-related events to RabbitMQ and a separate **NotificationService** that listens for those events.

Step 1: Setting Up RabbitMQ

If you haven't already, run RabbitMQ using Docker:

```bash
Copy code
docker run -d --hostname my-rabbit --name rabbitmq -p 5672:5672
-p 15672:15672 rabbitmq:3-management
```

Access the RabbitMQ management interface at http://localhost:15672 (default username/password: guest/guest).

Step 2: Publishing Events in ProductService

Modify the **ProductService** to publish events whenever a product is created or updated. Install the RabbitMQ.Client package:

```bash
Copy code
dotnet add package RabbitMQ.Client
```

Update the ProductController to include RabbitMQ publishing logic:

```csharp
Copy code
using RabbitMQ.Client;

[HttpPost]
public ActionResult<Product> CreateProduct(Product product)
{
    product.Id = products.Max(p => p.Id) + 1;
    products.Add(product);

    PublishProductEvent("ProductCreated", product);

    return CreatedAtAction(nameof(GetProduct), new { id =
    product.Id }, product);
}

private void PublishProductEvent(string eventType, Product
product)
{
    var factory = new ConnectionFactory { HostName = "localhost"
    };
    using var connection = factory.CreateConnection();
    using var channel = connection.CreateModel();

    channel.QueueDeclare(queue: "product_events", durable: false,
    exclusive: false, autoDelete: false, arguments: null);

    var message = JsonConvert.SerializeObject(new { EventType =
    eventType, Product = product });
    var body = Encoding.UTF8.GetBytes(message);

    channel.BasicPublish(exchange: "", routingKey:
    "product_events", basicProperties: null, body: body);
```

```
}
```

Step 3: Consuming Events in NotificationService

Create a new service called **NotificationService** that will listen for product events:

```bash
Copy code
dotnet new console -n NotificationService
cd NotificationService
dotnet add package RabbitMQ.Client
```

Implement the event listener in Program.cs:

```csharp
Copy code
using RabbitMQ.Client;
using RabbitMQ.Client.Events;
using System.Text;

var factory = new ConnectionFactory { HostName = "localhost" };
using var connection = factory.CreateConnection();
using var channel = connection.CreateModel();

channel.QueueDeclare(queue: "product_events", durable: false,
exclusive: false, autoDelete: false, arguments: null);

var consumer = new EventingBasicConsumer(channel);
consumer.Received += (model, ea) =>
{
    var body = ea.Body.ToArray();
    var message = Encoding.UTF8.GetString(body);
    var productEvent =
    JsonConvert.DeserializeObject<ProductEvent>(message);

    Console.WriteLine($"Received event: {productEvent.EventType}
    for Product ID: {productEvent.Product.Id}");
};
```

```
channel.BasicConsume(queue: "product_events", autoAck: true,
consumer: consumer);

Console.WriteLine("Waiting for product events...");
Console.ReadLine();

public class ProductEvent
{
    public string EventType { get; set; }
    public Product Product { get; set; }
}
```

Run both the **ProductService** and **NotificationService**, and whenever a product is created, the **NotificationService** will receive the event and log it to the console.

Section 4: Best Practices for Inter-Service Communication

As you design the communication between your microservices, it's important to adhere to certain best practices to ensure reliability, performance, and maintainability.

4.1 Use the Right Communication Protocol

Choosing the appropriate communication protocol is critical. Use REST for simple CRUD operations and gRPC for performance-critical services or where strong contracts are needed. Consider using message brokers for asynchronous processing or when you want to decouple services.

4.2 Handle Errors Gracefully

Implement error handling and resilience strategies, such as:

- **Retries**: Automatically retry failed requests.
- **Circuit Breakers**: Prevent repeated attempts to call a failing service.
- **Timeouts**: Set timeouts on service calls to prevent hanging requests.

4.3 Monitor and Log Communication

Monitoring and logging are essential to understanding how your microservices interact. Implement centralized logging and distributed tracing to capture and analyze communication flows. Use tools like **ELK Stack** or **Prometheus** for monitoring service health and performance.

4.4 Secure Communication

Ensure that communication between services is secure. Use HTTPS for REST APIs and secure your gRPC services with SSL/TLS. Implement authentication and authorization mechanisms to control access between services.

4.5 Document APIs

Documentation is crucial for APIs, especially in microservices architectures. Use tools like **Swagger** to auto-generate API documentation for RESTful services, and consider documenting your gRPC services using Protocol Buffers definitions.

Conclusion

In this chapter, we explored various inter-service communication mechanisms essential for building effective microservices:

- **RESTful APIs** provide a straightforward way to perform CRUD operations and are widely supported.
- **gRPC** offers high-performance communication with support for streaming and strongly typed contracts.
- **Message brokers** enable asynchronous communication and decoupling of services, facilitating event-driven architectures.

We also covered best practices for implementing effective communication between microservices, including choosing the right protocols, handling errors gracefully, monitoring and logging, securing communication, and documenting APIs. By mastering these concepts, you can create robust, efficient, and scalable microservices architectures that meet the demands of modern applications.

In the next chapter, we will delve into securing microservices, exploring authentication, authorization, and other critical security measures to ensure the integrity and confidentiality of your services.

Chapter 5: Securing Microservices

In a microservices architecture, security is paramount. As applications become more complex and distributed, the attack surface expands, making it crucial to implement robust security measures to protect services and data. This chapter will explore the various aspects of securing microservices, including authentication, authorization, secure communication, and best practices for ensuring that your microservices are safe from vulnerabilities.

By the end of this chapter, you will have a solid understanding of the security challenges associated with microservices and how to implement effective security measures using **C#12** and **.NET 8**.

Section 1: Understanding Security in Microservices

1.1 The Security Landscape of Microservices

Microservices introduce several security challenges compared to traditional monolithic applications, including:

- **Increased Attack Surface**: With multiple services communicating over a network, there are more points of entry for potential attacks.
- **Service-to-Service Communication**: Ensuring secure communication between services becomes critical, as services often need to authenticate and authorize each other.

- **Data Sensitivity**: Microservices often handle sensitive data that must be protected both in transit and at rest.
- **Distributed Nature**: The distributed nature of microservices complicates centralized security policies and monitoring.

1.2 Key Security Principles

To secure microservices effectively, organizations should adhere to several key security principles:

- **Least Privilege**: Grant the minimum necessary permissions for users and services to perform their tasks. This limits potential damage from compromised accounts.
- **Defense in Depth**: Implement multiple layers of security measures to protect your microservices, making it more difficult for attackers to penetrate the system.
- **Secure by Design**: Incorporate security considerations into the design phase of microservices development rather than treating it as an afterthought.
- **Regular Security Audits**: Perform regular security audits and assessments to identify vulnerabilities and ensure compliance with security policies.

Section 2: Authentication and Authorization

Authentication and authorization are fundamental aspects of securing microservices. Authentication verifies the identity of a user or service, while authorization determines whether the authenticated entity has permission to perform a specific action.

2.1 Authentication Strategies

There are several authentication strategies for microservices, including:

- **Basic Authentication**: A simple authentication scheme that uses a username and password encoded in the request header. It is easy to implement but not secure unless used with HTTPS.

- **Token-Based Authentication**: In this approach, the client receives a token after successful authentication, which is then included in subsequent requests. JSON Web Tokens (JWT) are commonly used for this purpose due to their compact size and ability to carry claims.
- **OAuth2**: A widely used authorization framework that enables third-party applications to obtain limited access to user accounts on an HTTP service. OAuth2 is often used in conjunction with OpenID Connect for user authentication.

Example: Implementing JWT Authentication in .NET 8

Let's implement JWT authentication in our **ProductService**.

1. **Install the Required Packages**:

```bash
Copy code
dotnet add package Microsoft.AspNetCore.
Authentication.JwtBearer
```

1. **Update appsettings.json with JWT Configuration**:

```json
Copy code
{
  "Jwt": {
    "Key": "YourSuperSecretKey",
    "Issuer": "YourIssuer",
    "Audience": "YourAudience"
  }
}
```

1. **Configure JWT Authentication in Program.cs**:

```csharp
Copy code
var builder = WebApplication.CreateBuilder(args);

builder.Services.AddAuthentication(options =>
{
    options.DefaultAuthenticateScheme =
    JwtBearerDefaults.AuthenticationScheme;
    options.DefaultChallengeScheme =
    JwtBearerDefaults.AuthenticationScheme;
})
.AddJwtBearer(options =>
{
    options.TokenValidationParameters =
 new TokenValidationParameters
    {
        ValidateIssuer = true,
        ValidateAudience = true,
        ValidateLifetime = true,
        ValidateIssuerSigningKey = true,
        ValidIssuer = builder.Configuration["Jwt:Issuer"],
        ValidAudience = builder.Configuration["Jwt:Audience"],
        IssuerSigningKey = new
SymmetricSecurityKey
(Encoding.UTF8.
GetBytes(builder
.Configuration["Jwt:Key"]))
    };
});

builder.Services.AddControllers();
var app = builder.Build();
app.UseAuthentication();
app.UseAuthorization();
app.MapControllers();
app.Run();
```

1. **Create a Token Generation Endpoint**: Add an endpoint to your controller for user authentication and token generation:

```csharp
Copy code
[HttpPost("authenticate")]
public IActionResult Authenticate
([FromBody] UserLogin userLogin)
{
    // Validate the user credentials (omitted for brevity)
    var tokenHandler = new JwtSecurityTokenHandler();
    var key = Encoding.ASCII.GetBytes(Configuration["Jwt:Key"]);
    var tokenDescriptor = new SecurityTokenDescriptor
    {
        Subject = new ClaimsIdentity(new[]
        {
            new Claim(ClaimTypes.Name, userLogin.Username)
        }),
        Expires = DateTime.UtcNow.AddHours(1),
        SigningCredentials = new
SigningCredentials
(new SymmetricSecurityKey(key),
SecurityAlgorithms.HmacSha256Signature)
    };

    var token = tokenHandler.CreateToken(tokenDescriptor);
    return Ok(new { Token = tokenHandler.WriteToken(token) });
}
```

With this setup, clients can obtain a JWT after authenticating and include it in subsequent requests using the Authorization header:

```css
Copy code
Authorization: Bearer {token}
```

2.2 Authorization Mechanisms

Authorization determines what authenticated users or services are allowed to do. Common authorization mechanisms include:

- **Role-Based Access Control (RBAC)**: Users are assigned to roles, and permissions are granted to those roles. This simplifies permission management.
- **Attribute-Based Access Control (ABAC)**: Access is granted based on attributes (user attributes, resource attributes, environment conditions) rather than roles.

Example: Implementing Role-Based Authorization in .NET 8
You can define roles and use them for authorization in your application.

1. **Update the UserLogin Model**:

```csharp
Copy code
public class UserLogin
{
    public string Username { get; set; }
    public string Password { get; set; }
    public string Role { get; set; } // Add role property
}
```

1. **Authorize Roles in Controller**: Use the [Authorize] attribute to secure your endpoints:

```csharp
Copy code
[Authorize(Roles = "Admin")]
[HttpPost("create")]
public IActionResult CreateProduct(Product product)
```

```
{
    // Product creation logic
}
```

In this example, only users with the Admin role can access the CreateProduct endpoint.

Section 3: Secure Communication

Securing communication between microservices is vital to protect sensitive data and prevent unauthorized access. The two main aspects to consider are transport security and message security.

3.1 Transport Security

Transport security ensures that data is encrypted during transmission. For microservices, this typically involves using HTTPS or TLS to secure HTTP communication.

- **HTTPS**: Using HTTPS ensures that all data exchanged between services is encrypted. Configure your services to use SSL certificates to enable HTTPS.

Example: Enabling HTTPS in .NET 8

.NET 8 provides built-in support for HTTPS. You can configure your project to enforce HTTPS by modifying the launchSettings.json file:

```json
Copy code
"profiles": {
    "IIS Express": {
        "commandName": "IISExpress",
        "launchBrowser": true,
        "environmentVariables": {
            "ASPNETCORE_ENVIRONMENT": "Development"
        }
```

```
        },
        "ProductService": {
            "commandName": "Project",
            "launchBrowser": true,
            "applicationUrl":
            "https://localhost:5001;http://localhost:5000",
            "environmentVariables": {
                "ASPNETCORE_ENVIRONMENT": "Development"
            }
        }
    }
}
```

Run your application, and it will listen on both HTTP and HTTPS endpoints.

3.2 Message Security

In addition to securing transport, it's essential to ensure that the messages exchanged between services are secure. This includes signing and encrypting messages.

- **Message Signing**: Sign messages using cryptographic keys to ensure the integrity and authenticity of the data.
- **Message Encryption**: Encrypt sensitive data before transmitting it, ensuring that only authorized parties can decrypt and access the information.

Example: Securing Messages with JSON Web Tokens

When using JWT for authentication, you inherently gain some level of message security. The JWT can be signed and encrypted, ensuring that only the intended recipient can read the payload.

To implement message signing in .NET, ensure that you use a strong signing algorithm (e.g., RS256) and securely store your private keys.

Section 4: Best Practices for Securing Microservices

To effectively secure your microservices architecture, adhere to the following best practices:

4.1 Secure the API Gateway

As the entry point to your microservices, the API Gateway should implement security measures such as:

- **Authentication and Authorization**: Validate incoming requests and enforce permissions.
- **Rate Limiting**: Protect services from excessive requests by limiting the number of requests from a single client.
- **Input Validation**: Validate and sanitize all incoming data to prevent injection attacks.

4.2 Implement Centralized Logging and Monitoring

Set up centralized logging and monitoring solutions to capture security events and anomalies. Use tools like **ELK Stack**, **Azure Monitor**, or **Prometheus** to collect and analyze logs.

4.3 Regularly Update Dependencies

Keep your microservices' dependencies up to date to mitigate vulnerabilities. Regularly scan for known vulnerabilities using tools like **OWASP Dependency-Check**.

4.4 Conduct Security Audits and Penetration Testing

Perform regular security audits and penetration testing to identify and remediate potential vulnerabilities. Engage security experts to assess your microservices architecture.

4.5 Implement Network Security

Use firewalls and security groups to restrict access to your microservices. Ensure that only necessary ports are open and limit access to trusted IP addresses.

Section 5: Case Study: Securing a Sample Microservices Application

Let's walk through a case study of a sample microservices application that implements the security measures discussed in this chapter. The application consists of a **ProductService**, **OrderService**, and **NotificationService**.

5.1 Application Overview

- **ProductService**: Manages products and exposes a RESTful API and gRPC service for product operations.
- **OrderService**: Processes orders and communicates with the **ProductService** for product information.
- **NotificationService**: Sends notifications based on events published by the **ProductService**.

5.2 Security Architecture

1. **API Gateway**: All requests to the microservices pass through the API Gateway, which handles authentication and authorization.
2. **JWT Authentication**: The API Gateway issues JWT tokens for authenticated users, which are used for subsequent requests.
3. **Service Communication**: Secure communication is enforced using HTTPS, and messages between services are encrypted.
4. **Centralized Logging**: All security events are logged centrally for monitoring and auditing.
5. 3 Implementation Steps
6. **Set Up API Gateway**: Configure the API Gateway to handle authentication, route requests to microservices, and apply rate limiting.
7. **Implement JWT Authentication**: Set up the authentication mechanism in the API Gateway and ensure all microservices validate incoming tokens.
8. **Secure Microservices**: Enable HTTPS for all services and implement authorization checks in each service.
9. **Deploy and Monitor**: Deploy the application and configure central-

ized logging and monitoring solutions.

Conclusion

Securing microservices is a multifaceted challenge that requires a comprehensive approach. In this chapter, we explored the various aspects of microservices security, including authentication, authorization, secure communication, and best practices.

Key takeaways include:

- Implementing robust authentication and authorization mechanisms using JWT and OAuth2.
- Ensuring secure communication between microservices using HTTPS and message security.
- Adhering to best practices such as centralized logging, regular updates, and security audits.

By applying these principles and practices, you can create a secure microservices architecture that protects your applications and data from vulnerabilities and attacks. In the next chapter, we will dive into deploying microservices to cloud environments, exploring containerization, orchestration, and CI/CD pipelines for efficient deployment and scaling.

Chapter 6: Deploying Microservices in the Cloud

As microservices architecture gains traction, deploying these services effectively in cloud environments becomes paramount. Cloud platforms offer flexibility, scalability, and resource efficiency, making them an ideal choice for deploying microservices. This chapter will provide a comprehensive guide on deploying microservices in the cloud, covering key topics such as containerization, orchestration, continuous integration and deployment (CI/CD) pipelines, and best practices to ensure successful deployment.

By the end of this chapter, you will have a solid understanding of how to deploy your microservices in cloud environments, leverage containerization technologies like Docker, orchestrate your services with Kubernetes, and implement CI/CD pipelines to streamline your development workflow.

Section 1: Introduction to Cloud Deployment

1.1 Why Deploy Microservices in the Cloud?
Deploying microservices in the cloud provides several advantages:

- **Scalability**: Cloud providers offer automatic scaling capabilities, allowing you to handle varying loads by adjusting resources dynamically.

- **Cost Efficiency**: With pay-as-you-go pricing models, you only pay for the resources you use, helping to optimize costs.
- **Reliability**: Leading cloud platforms offer high availability and redundancy, minimizing downtime and ensuring that your services remain accessible.
- **Resource Management**: Cloud environments abstract infrastructure management, enabling teams to focus on application development instead of managing servers.

1.2 Cloud Deployment Models
There are various cloud deployment models available:

- **Public Cloud**: Services are hosted on third-party cloud providers like AWS, Azure, and Google Cloud, allowing users to access resources over the internet.
- **Private Cloud**: Resources are dedicated to a single organization, providing enhanced security and control.
- **Hybrid Cloud**: Combines public and private clouds, allowing organizations to manage sensitive data in a private cloud while leveraging the scalability of the public cloud.

Section 2: Containerization with Docker

2.1 What is Containerization?
Containerization is the practice of packaging applications and their dependencies into isolated units called **containers**. Containers are lightweight, portable, and can run consistently across different environments.
2.2 Benefits of Containerization

- **Consistency**: Containers ensure that applications run the same way in development, testing, and production environments, reducing the "it works on my machine" problem.
- **Isolation**: Each container runs independently, allowing multiple ser-

vices to coexist on the same host without conflicts.

- **Portability**: Containers can be easily moved between different environments (e.g., from a developer's machine to the cloud) without modification.

2.3 Setting Up Docker for Microservices

Step 1: Installing Docker

To get started with Docker, you need to install it on your machine. Follow these steps:

1. Download Docker from the official Docker website.
2. Follow the installation instructions for your operating system (Windows, macOS, or Linux).
3. After installation, verify that Docker is running by executing the following command in your terminal:

```bash
Copy code
docker --version
```

Step 2: Creating a Dockerfile

A **Dockerfile** is a script that contains instructions for building a Docker image. Let's create a Dockerfile for the **ProductService**:

1. In the root of your **ProductService** project, create a file named Dockerfile and add the following content:

```dockerfile
Copy code
# Use the official .NET SDK as the build environment
FROM mcr.microsoft.com/dotnet/sdk:8.0 AS build
```

```
WORKDIR /app
COPY . .
RUN dotnet restore
RUN dotnet publish -c Release -o out

# Use the official .NET runtime as the final base image
FROM mcr.microsoft.com/dotnet/aspnet:8.0
WORKDIR /app
COPY --from=build /app/out .
ENTRYPOINT ["dotnet", "ProductService.dll"]
```

This Dockerfile performs the following tasks:

- Uses the .NET SDK image for the build environment.
- Copies the project files, restores dependencies, and publishes the application to the out directory.
- Uses the .NET runtime image as the base for the final container, copying the published output and setting the entry point.

Step 3: Building the Docker Image

To build the Docker image for your microservice, run the following command in your terminal:

```bash
Copy code
docker build -t productservice .
```

This command builds a Docker image named productservice based on the Dockerfile in the current directory.

Step 4: Running the Docker Container

Once the image is built, you can run it as a container:

```bash
Copy code
docker run -d -p 5000:80 --name productservice productservice
```

This command runs the productservice container in detached mode, mapping port 80 in the container to port 5000 on your host.

You can now access the service at http://localhost:5000/api/products.

Section 3: Orchestrating Microservices with Kubernetes

3.1 What is Kubernetes?

Kubernetes (often abbreviated as K8s) is an open-source container orchestration platform that automates the deployment, scaling, and management of containerized applications. It allows you to manage multiple containers across a cluster of machines, providing features like load balancing, service discovery, and self-healing.

3.2 Benefits of Using Kubernetes

- **Automated Deployment and Scaling**: Kubernetes automates the deployment of containerized applications, scaling them up or down based on demand.
- **Load Balancing**: K8s can automatically distribute traffic across multiple instances of a service, ensuring high availability and reliability.
- **Self-Healing**: If a container fails, Kubernetes automatically restarts or replaces it, maintaining the desired state of the application.
- **Rolling Updates and Rollbacks**: Kubernetes supports rolling updates, allowing you to deploy new versions of applications with minimal downtime.

3.3 Setting Up Kubernetes

To deploy your microservices with Kubernetes, you need to set up a Kubernetes cluster. You can use services like **Azure Kubernetes Service (AKS)**, **Google Kubernetes Engine (GKE)**, or **Amazon Elastic Kubernetes**

Service (EKS). For local development, you can use **Minikube** or **Docker Desktop** with Kubernetes enabled.

Step 1: Installing Minikube

To get started with Minikube, follow these steps:

1. Install **Minikube** by following the instructions on the official Minikube website.
2. Start Minikube:

```bash
Copy code
minikube start
```

1. Verify that Minikube is running:

```bash
Copy code
kubectl get nodes
```

Step 2: Deploying the ProductService to Kubernetes

To deploy your microservice to Kubernetes, you need to create a Kubernetes deployment and service.

1. Create a file named productservice-deployment.yaml with the following content:

```yaml
Copy code
```

```
apiVersion: apps/v1
kind: Deployment
metadata:
  name: productservice
spec:
  replicas: 3
  selector:
    matchLabels:
      app: productservice
  template:
    metadata:
      labels:
        app: productservice
    spec:
      containers:
        - name: productservice
          image: productservice:latest
          ports:
            - containerPort: 80
```

1. Create a file named productservice-service.yaml with the following content:

```
yaml
Copy code
apiVersion: v1
kind: Service
metadata:
  name: productservice
spec:
  type: LoadBalancer
  ports:
    - port: 80
      targetPort: 80
  selector:
    app: productservice
```

1. Apply the deployment and service to your Minikube cluster:

```bash
Copy code
kubectl apply -f productservice-deployment.yaml
kubectl apply -f productservice-service.yaml
```

1. Verify that your service is running:

```bash
Copy code
kubectl get deployments
kubectl get services
```

1. Access the service using Minikube's service command:

```bash
Copy code
minikube service productservice
```

This command will open the service in your default web browser, allowing you to interact with the deployed microservice.

Section 4: Continuous Integration and Continuous Deployment (CI/CD)

4.1 What is CI/CD?

Continuous Integration (CI) and **Continuous Deployment (CD)** are practices that automate the integration and deployment of code changes into production environments. CI/CD pipelines streamline the development process, allowing teams to deliver features and fixes faster and more reliably.

4.2 Benefits of CI/CD

- **Faster Development Cycles**: Automating testing and deployment processes accelerates the delivery of new features and updates.
- **Improved Quality**: Automated tests ensure that new changes do not introduce bugs or regressions.
- **Consistent Deployments**: CI/CD pipelines help ensure consistent and repeatable deployments, reducing the risk of errors during deployment.

4.3 Implementing CI/CD with GitHub Actions

Let's implement a CI/CD pipeline using **GitHub Actions** to automate the build and deployment of the **ProductService**.

Step 1: Creating a GitHub Actions Workflow

In your **ProductService** repository, create a folder named .github/workflows and add a new file named ci-cd.yml:

```yaml
yaml
Copy code
name: CI/CD Pipeline

on:
  push:
    branches:
      - main

jobs:
```

```
build:
  runs-on: ubuntu-latest
  steps:
    - name: Checkout code
      uses: actions/checkout@v2

    - name: Set up .NET
      uses: actions/setup-dotnet@v1
      with:
        dotnet-version: '8.0.x'

    - name: Restore dependencies
      run: dotnet restore

    - name: Build
      run: dotnet build --configuration Release --no-restore

    - name: Test
      run: dotnet test --no-build --verbosity normal

    - name: Build Docker image
      run: |
        docker build . -t
        your-dockerhub-username/productservice:latest
        echo "${{ secrets.DOCKER_PASSWORD }}" | docker login -u
        "${{ secrets.DOCKER_USERNAME }}" --password-stdin
        docker push
        your-dockerhub-username/productservice:latest

deploy:
  runs-on: ubuntu-latest
  needs: build
  steps:
    - name: Deploy to Kubernetes
      run: |
        kubectl set image deployment/productservice
        productservice=your-dockerhub-username/productservice:latest
```

This GitHub Actions workflow performs the following tasks:

- Triggers on push events to the main branch.
- Checks out the code and sets up the .NET environment.
- Restores dependencies, builds the application, and runs tests.
- Builds the Docker image and pushes it to Docker Hub.
- Deploys the latest image to the Kubernetes cluster.

Step 2: Setting Up Secrets

In your GitHub repository, navigate to **Settings > Secrets** and add the following secrets:

- **DOCKER_USERNAME**: Your Docker Hub username.
- **DOCKER_PASSWORD**: Your Docker Hub password.

With this setup, every time you push code to the main branch, the CI/CD pipeline will run, building and deploying your microservice automatically.

Section 5: Best Practices for Deploying Microservices

To ensure successful deployment of microservices in the cloud, adhere to the following best practices:

5.1 Monitor and Log Microservices

Implement monitoring and logging solutions to track the health and performance of your microservices. Use tools like **Prometheus**, **Grafana**, and **ELK Stack** for observability.

5.2 Implement Health Checks

Use health checks to ensure that your microservices are running properly. Kubernetes supports liveness and readiness probes that can automatically restart unhealthy containers.

5.3 Use Infrastructure as Code (IaC)

Adopt IaC practices to manage and provision your infrastructure using code. Tools like **Terraform**, **AWS CloudFormation**, or **Azure Resource Manager** templates allow you to automate the setup and configuration of cloud resources.

5.4 Ensure Data Management Strategies

Implement strategies for managing data across microservices, including:

- **Database per Service**: Each microservice should have its own database to ensure independence.
- **Event Sourcing**: Capture all changes to application state as events, allowing you to reconstruct the current state from the event store.

5.5 Plan for Scaling

Consider how your microservices will scale based on demand. Use horizontal scaling to add more instances of your services as needed, and leverage cloud provider features for auto-scaling.

Conclusion

In this chapter, we explored the entire process of deploying microservices in the cloud. Key topics covered include:

- **Containerization** with Docker to package microservices for deployment.
- **Orchestration** with Kubernetes to manage containerized applications.
- **Continuous Integration and Continuous Deployment (CI/CD)** pipelines to automate the build and deployment processes.

By implementing these practices, you can effectively deploy your microservices in cloud environments, ensuring scalability, reliability, and maintainability. In the next chapter, we will delve into monitoring and managing microservices, exploring strategies for observability, health checks, and performance tuning.

Chapter 7: Monitoring and Managing Microservices

I n the realm of microservices architecture, monitoring and management are critical to ensuring the health, performance, and reliability of distributed systems. As microservices communicate over networks and run in dynamic environments, gaining visibility into their operation becomes essential for quick troubleshooting and maintaining service quality. This chapter will explore the best practices for monitoring and managing microservices, including key concepts such as observability, logging, metrics, health checks, and performance tuning.

By the end of this chapter, you will have a solid understanding of how to effectively monitor and manage your microservices to enhance their performance and resilience.

Section 1: The Importance of Monitoring in Microservices

1.1 Understanding Observability

Observability refers to the ability to understand the internal state of a system based on the data it generates. In microservices, observability is crucial for diagnosing issues, understanding performance, and ensuring that services function as expected.

Observability can be broken down into three key pillars:

- **Metrics**: Numerical data that provides insights into system performance (e.g., CPU usage, request latency).
- **Logs**: Textual records that capture events that occur within the system, providing context for troubleshooting.
- **Tracing**: Information about the flow of requests through the system, helping to identify bottlenecks and dependencies between services.

1.2 Benefits of Monitoring Microservices

Effective monitoring provides numerous benefits:

- **Proactive Issue Detection**: By continuously monitoring services, you can detect issues before they affect users.
- **Improved Performance**: Monitoring helps identify performance bottlenecks and allows for optimizations.
- **Enhanced Reliability**: Understanding the health of services enables you to maintain higher availability and reduce downtime.
- **Informed Decision-Making**: Data from monitoring tools can inform capacity planning and architectural decisions.

Section 2: Key Metrics for Monitoring Microservices

2.1 Identifying Essential Metrics

When monitoring microservices, it's vital to track key performance indicators (KPIs) that reflect the health and performance of the services. Common metrics include:

- **Response Time**: The time taken to process a request, indicating how quickly services respond.
- **Error Rate**: The percentage of failed requests compared to total requests, providing insights into service reliability.
- **Throughput**: The number of requests processed in a given time period, indicating the system's capacity.
- **Resource Utilization**: Metrics related to CPU, memory, disk, and

network usage, helping identify resource constraints.

2.2 Implementing Metrics Collection

You can use libraries and frameworks to collect and expose metrics for your microservices. One popular option is **Prometheus**, an open-source monitoring and alerting toolkit.

Step 1: Installing Prometheus

1. Install Prometheus on your local machine or use a managed instance from a cloud provider.
2. Create a configuration file named prometheus.yml:

```yaml
Copy code
global:
  scrape_interval: 15s

scrape_configs:
  - job_name: 'productservice'
    static_configs:
      - targets: ['localhost:5000']
```

Step 2: Exposing Metrics in .NET 8

In your **ProductService**, install the **Prometheus.AspNetCore** NuGet package:

```bash
Copy code
dotnet add package prometheus-net.AspNetCore
```

Next, update the Program.cs file to expose Prometheus metrics:

```csharp
csharp
Copy code
using Prometheus;

var builder = WebApplication.CreateBuilder(args);

builder.Services.AddControllers();

var app = builder.Build();

app.UseRouting();
app.UseHttpMetrics();

app.MapGet("/metrics", async context =>
{
    await context.Response.WriteAsync
(Prometheus.Metrics.DefaultRegistry.
CollectAll().ToString());
});

app.MapControllers();
app.Run();
```

With this setup, Prometheus will scrape metrics from the /metrics endpoint every 15 seconds.

Section 3: Logging in Microservices

3.1 The Role of Logging

Logging is essential for troubleshooting issues and gaining insights into system behavior. In microservices, logging must be handled effectively to provide useful information without overwhelming the system.

3.2 Types of Logs

Different types of logs can be useful in microservices:

- **Application Logs**: Log messages generated by the application itself, capturing events, errors, and important state changes.

- **Access Logs**: Log incoming requests and their responses, including timestamps, IP addresses, and response statuses.
- **Error Logs**: Capture exceptions and error messages, providing critical information for diagnosing issues.

3.3 Implementing Structured Logging

Structured logging involves logging data in a structured format (e.g., JSON), making it easier to query and analyze logs.

Step 1: Using Serilog for Structured Logging

Install the **Serilog** package along with the Serilog.AspNetCore and Serilog.Sinks.Console packages:

```bash
Copy code
dotnet add package Serilog.AspNetCore
dotnet add package Serilog.Sinks.Console
```

Step 2: Configuring Serilog in Program.cs

Update your Program.cs to set up Serilog:

```csharp
Copy code
using Serilog;

var builder = WebApplication.CreateBuilder(args);

Log.Logger = new LoggerConfiguration()
    .WriteTo.Console()
    .CreateLogger();

builder.Host.UseSerilog();

builder.Services.AddControllers();
var app = builder.Build();

app.UseRouting();
```

```
app.UseHttpMetrics();
app.UseAuthorization();

app.MapControllers();
app.Run();
```

Step 3: Logging Events in the Controller

Use logging in your controllers to capture important events:

```csharp
Copy code
using Microsoft.AspNetCore.Mvc;
using Serilog;

[ApiController]
[Route("api/products")]
public class ProductController : ControllerBase
{
    [HttpPost]
    public ActionResult<Product>
CreateProduct(Product product)
    {
        Log.Information("Creating product: {ProductName}",
        product.Name);
        // Create product logic
        return CreatedAtAction
(nameof(GetProduct), new
{ id = product.Id }, product);
    }
}
```

By implementing structured logging with Serilog, you can effectively log and analyze events in your microservices.

Section 4: Tracing Requests Between Microservices

4.1 Understanding Distributed Tracing

Distributed tracing is a technique used to track requests as they flow through multiple services in a microservices architecture. It helps identify latency issues, bottlenecks, and dependencies between services.

4.2 Implementing Distributed Tracing with OpenTelemetry

OpenTelemetry is an open-source observability framework that provides APIs and libraries for collecting telemetry data from applications.

Step 1: Installing OpenTelemetry

Install the required packages in your microservices:

```bash
Copy code
dotnet add package OpenTelemetry
dotnet add package OpenTelemetry.Exporter.Console
```

Step 2: Configuring OpenTelemetry in Program.cs

Set up OpenTelemetry to collect traces:

```csharp
Copy code
using OpenTelemetry;
using OpenTelemetry.Resources;

var builder = WebApplication.
CreateBuilder(args);

// Add OpenTelemetry tracing
builder.Services.AddOpenTelemetryTracing
(tracerProviderBuilder =>
{
    tracerProviderBuilder
        .SetResourceBuilder
(ResourceBuilder.
CreateDefault().AddService
```

```
("ProductService"))
        .AddAspNetCoreInstrumentation()
        .AddConsoleExporter();
});

builder.Services.AddControllers();
var app = builder.Build();

app.MapControllers();
app.Run();
```

Step 3: Analyzing Traces

With OpenTelemetry set up, traces will be collected and printed to the console. You can analyze these traces to understand the flow of requests and identify any performance issues.

Section 5: Health Checks and Resilience

5.1 The Importance of Health Checks

Health checks are essential for ensuring that your microservices are running correctly and can handle requests. Health checks can be used by orchestration tools like Kubernetes to monitor service health and take corrective action if a service becomes unhealthy.

5.2 Implementing Health Checks in .NET 8

In .NET 8, you can easily implement health checks using the built-in health check middleware.

Step 1: Adding Health Check Services

In your Program.cs, add health check services:

```
csharp
Copy code
builder.Services.AddHealthChecks();
```

Step 2: Configuring Health Check Endpoints

Add health check endpoints to your application:

```csharp
Copy code
app.MapHealthChecks("/health");
```

Step 3: Testing Health Checks

Run your application and access the health check endpoint:

```bash
Copy code
http://localhost:5000/health
```

You should receive a response indicating the health status of your microservice.

Section 6: Performance Tuning in Microservices

6.1 Understanding Performance Metrics

Performance tuning involves optimizing your microservices to handle increased load while maintaining responsiveness. Key performance metrics to monitor include:

- **Latency**: The time taken to process requests.
- **Throughput**: The number of requests handled in a given time period.
- **Resource Utilization**: CPU, memory, and network usage.

6.2 Optimizing Performance in .NET 8

Here are some techniques to optimize performance in your .NET 8 microservices:

Step 1: Asynchronous Programming

Use asynchronous programming to improve responsiveness and scalability. For example, modify your API methods to be asynchronous:

```csharp
Copy code
[HttpGet("{id}")]
public async Task<ActionResult<Product>>
GetProductAsync(int id)
{
    var product = await _productRepository.
GetProductAsync(id);
    if (product == null) return NotFound();
    return Ok(product);
}
```

Step 2: Caching Responses

Implement caching to reduce the load on your microservices. You can use in-memory caching or distributed caching solutions like Redis.

1. Install the necessary package:

```bash
Copy code
dotnet add package Microsoft.
Extensions.Caching.Memory
```

1. Configure caching in your Program.cs:

```csharp
Copy code
builder.Services.AddMemoryCache();
```

1. Use caching in your controller:

```csharp
Copy code
[HttpGet("{id}")]
public ActionResult<Product> GetProduct(int id)
{
    if (_cache.TryGetValue($"product-{id}",
 out Product product))
    {
        return Ok(product);
    }

    product = _productRepository.GetProduct(id);
    if (product == null) return NotFound();

    _cache.Set($"product-{id}", product,
TimeSpan.FromMinutes(5));
    return Ok(product);
}
```

Step 3: Database Optimization

Optimize your database interactions by using efficient queries, indexing, and connection pooling. Consider using **Entity Framework Core** to manage database interactions more effectively.

Section 7: Case Study: Monitoring and Managing a Microservices Application

Let's walk through a case study of monitoring and managing a microservices application that includes the **ProductService**, **OrderService**, and **NotificationService**.

7.1 Application Overview

- **ProductService**: Manages product information and exposes a RESTful API for clients.
- **OrderService**: Processes orders and communicates with the **Product-**

100

Service to fetch product details.
- **NotificationService**: Sends notifications based on events published by the **ProductService**.

7.2 Security Architecture

1. **Observability**: Implemented metrics collection using Prometheus, logging with Serilog, and distributed tracing with OpenTelemetry.
2. **Health Checks**: Health check endpoints are configured for each service to monitor their status.
3. **Resilience**: Circuit Breaker pattern is applied to the **OrderService** to handle failures gracefully when communicating with the **ProductService**.

7.3 Implementation Steps

1. **Set Up Monitoring**: Configure Prometheus to scrape metrics from all microservices and set up Grafana for visualization.
2. **Implement Logging**: Use Serilog to log events and errors across services, enabling easy troubleshooting.
3. **Set Up Health Checks**: Add health check endpoints to each service and configure Kubernetes to manage service availability based on health status.
4. **Optimize Performance**: Monitor performance metrics, identify bottlenecks, and implement optimizations as needed.

Conclusion

In this chapter, we explored the critical aspects of monitoring and managing microservices, including:

- **Observability** and the key pillars of metrics, logging, and tracing.
- **Health checks** to ensure service availability and performance.

- **Performance tuning** techniques to optimize microservices for scalability and responsiveness.

By implementing these practices, you can gain valuable insights into the operation of your microservices, allowing you to respond quickly to issues and maintain high service quality. In the next chapter, we will explore strategies for scaling microservices, including horizontal and vertical scaling, load balancing, and managing state in a distributed architecture.

Chapter 8: Scaling Microservices

S caling is a fundamental aspect of microservices architecture, enabling applications to handle increasing loads and providing resilience against failures. As applications grow and evolve, they must adapt to changing demands while maintaining performance, reliability, and cost-effectiveness. This chapter will explore various strategies for scaling microservices, including both horizontal and vertical scaling, load balancing, managing state, and leveraging cloud-native services.

By the end of this chapter, you will have a comprehensive understanding of how to scale your microservices effectively and efficiently.

Section 1: Understanding Scaling in Microservices

1.1 Why Scale Microservices?

Microservices architectures are designed to be modular and independently deployable, making them inherently more scalable than monolithic applications. However, scaling is crucial for several reasons:

- **Increased Demand**: As user demand grows, applications must be able to handle larger volumes of traffic without compromising performance.
- **Resource Optimization**: Efficient scaling allows organizations to optimize their resource usage, reducing costs while maintaining service quality.

- **Improved Resilience**: Scaling can enhance the resilience of applications, distributing workloads across multiple instances to prevent downtime.

1.2 Types of Scaling

There are two primary types of scaling in microservices:

- **Horizontal Scaling (Scaling Out)**: Adding more instances of a service to handle increased load. This approach distributes incoming requests across multiple instances, improving throughput and fault tolerance.
- **Vertical Scaling (Scaling Up)**: Increasing the resources (CPU, memory) of an existing instance. While this can improve performance, it is often limited by the capacity of the underlying hardware and can lead to single points of failure.

Section 2: Horizontal Scaling

2.1 Implementing Horizontal Scaling

Horizontal scaling is typically the preferred method for scaling microservices, as it provides better resilience and can handle larger loads. Here are some techniques to implement horizontal scaling:

Step 1: Deploying Multiple Instances

To horizontally scale a microservice, you can deploy multiple instances of the service behind a load balancer. Each instance can handle a portion of the incoming traffic, distributing the load effectively.

1. **Docker Swarm**: Use Docker Swarm to manage and orchestrate your containers. You can define services with a specified number of replicas to achieve horizontal scaling.

```bash
bash
Copy code
docker service create --replicas 3 --name productservice
your-dockerhub-username/productservice
```

1. **Kubernetes**: Use Kubernetes to manage and scale your microservices. You can define the number of replicas in your deployment configuration:

```yaml
yaml
Copy code
apiVersion: apps/v1
kind: Deployment
metadata:
  name: productservice
spec:
  replicas: 3
  template:
    metadata:
      labels:
        app: productservice
    spec:
      containers:
        - name: productservice
          image: your-dockerhub-username/productservice:latest
          ports:
            - containerPort: 80
```

Step 2: Using Load Balancers

Load balancers distribute incoming requests across multiple service instances, ensuring that no single instance becomes a bottleneck.

1. **Kubernetes Load Balancer**: In Kubernetes, you can create a service of type LoadBalancer to automatically provision an external load balancer that routes traffic to your service instances.

```yaml
yaml
Copy code
apiVersion: v1
kind: Service
metadata:
  name: productservice
spec:
  type: LoadBalancer
  ports:
    - port: 80
      targetPort: 80
  selector:
    app: productservice
```

1. **Cloud Load Balancers**: Use cloud provider load balancers (e.g., AWS Elastic Load Balancer, Azure Load Balancer) to route traffic to multiple instances of your services.

Step 3: Auto-Scaling

Auto-scaling allows your application to automatically adjust the number of running instances based on predefined metrics, such as CPU usage or request latency.

1. **Kubernetes Horizontal Pod Autoscaler (HPA)**: In Kubernetes, you can configure HPA to automatically scale the number of pods in a deployment based on metrics.

```yaml
yaml
Copy code
apiVersion: autoscaling/v2beta2
kind: HorizontalPodAutoscaler
metadata:
```

```
  name: productservice-hpa
spec:
  scaleTargetRef:
    apiVersion: apps/v1
    kind: Deployment
    name: productservice
  minReplicas: 3
  maxReplicas: 10
  metrics:
    - type: Resource
      resource:
        name: cpu
        target:
          type: Utilization
          averageUtilization: 50
```

This configuration will automatically scale the number of productservice pods based on CPU utilization.

Section 3: Vertical Scaling

3.1 When to Use Vertical Scaling
  Vertical scaling is useful in certain scenarios:

- When specific workloads require more resources (e.g., heavy computation tasks).
- During the initial stages of development, when rapid scaling is not yet needed.
- For legacy applications that may not be easily containerized or orchestrated.

However, vertical scaling has limitations:

- Physical limits: You can only scale up to the maximum capacity of the underlying hardware.
- Risk of single points of failure: If the single instance fails, the service

becomes unavailable.

3.2 Implementing Vertical Scaling in .NET 8
If you decide to implement vertical scaling, here are a few techniques:

1. **Increase Resources on Cloud Instances**: Most cloud providers allow you to change the instance type of your service to one with more CPU and memory resources. For example, in AWS, you can modify the instance type in the EC2 console.
2. **Optimize Application Performance**: Review and optimize your application code and database queries to improve performance without needing to scale up hardware.
3. **Use Connection Pooling**: If your microservice interacts with databases, use connection pooling to manage database connections more efficiently.

Section 4: Load Balancing Strategies

4.1 Overview of Load Balancing
Load balancing is the distribution of network traffic across multiple servers or instances to ensure no single server becomes overwhelmed. Proper load balancing improves resource utilization, minimizes response time, and enhances application reliability.

4.2 Load Balancing Algorithms
Several algorithms can be used for load balancing:

- **Round Robin**: Distributes requests sequentially to each instance.
- **Least Connections**: Routes traffic to the instance with the fewest active connections.
- **IP Hash**: Directs requests from a specific IP address to the same server for session persistence.

4.3 Implementing Load Balancing

Load balancing can be implemented at various levels:

1. **Client-Side Load Balancing**: Clients use load balancers to distribute requests among instances. Libraries like **Ribbon** (for Java) or **Steeltoe** (for .NET) can be used for client-side load balancing.
2. **Server-Side Load Balancing**: Use dedicated load balancers to manage traffic, such as:

- **Nginx**: Can be configured as a reverse proxy and load balancer for your microservices.
- **HAProxy**: A high-performance TCP/HTTP load balancer that can distribute requests efficiently.

Example: Configuring Nginx as a Load Balancer

1. Install Nginx on your server.
2. Create a configuration file (nginx.conf) with the following content:

```nginx
Copy code
http {
    upstream productservice {
        server productservice1:80;
        server productservice2:80;
        server productservice3:80;
    }

    server {
        listen 80;

        location / {
            proxy_pass http://productservice;
        }
    }
```

```
}
```

This configuration routes incoming requests to the defined productservice upstream servers.

Section 5: Managing State in Microservices

5.1 The Challenge of Managing State

In microservices architecture, managing state is a complex issue due to the distributed nature of services. Each microservice should ideally remain stateless to enhance scalability and reliability.

- **Stateless Services**: A stateless service does not store any data about client sessions. Each request is treated independently, which simplifies scaling.

5.2 Strategies for State Management

When state management is necessary, consider the following strategies:

1. **Database per Service**: Each microservice should have its own database to manage its state independently, allowing for better decoupling.
2. **External Storage Solutions**: Use external systems like **Redis, Memcached**, or cloud-native databases (e.g., **Amazon DynamoDB, Azure Cosmos DB**) for managing stateful data.
3. **Event Sourcing**: Capture all changes to an application's state as a sequence of events, allowing you to rebuild the current state from these events.
4. **CQRS (Command Query Responsibility Segregation)**: Separate read and write operations to manage state more effectively, especially when dealing with high-read scenarios.

Example: Implementing State Management with Redis

1. **Installing Redis**: Run Redis using Docker:

```bash
Copy code
docker run -d -p 6379:6379 --name redis redis
```

1. **Using Redis in Your Microservice**:
2. Install the necessary package:

```bash
Copy code
dotnet add package StackExchange.Redis
```

1. Use Redis in your microservice for state management:

```csharp
Copy code
var redis = ConnectionMultiplexer.Connect("localhost");
var db = redis.GetDatabase();

// Set a value
db.StringSet("product:1", JsonConvert.SerializeObject(product));

// Get a value
var productData = db.StringGet("product:1");
var product = JsonConvert.DeserializeObject<Product>(productData);
```

Section 6: Case Study: Scaling a Microservices Application

Let's explore a case study of scaling a microservices application that includes the **ProductService, OrderService**, and **NotificationService**.

6.1 Application Overview

- **ProductService**: Manages product information.
- **OrderService**: Processes orders and communicates with the **Product-Service**.
- **NotificationService**: Sends notifications based on events.

6.2 Scaling Strategy

1. **Horizontal Scaling**: Deploy multiple instances of each service behind a load balancer to handle increased traffic.
2. **Load Balancing**: Use Kubernetes' built-in load balancer to distribute requests evenly among service instances.
3. **Auto-Scaling**: Implement Kubernetes Horizontal Pod Autoscaler (HPA) to automatically adjust the number of service instances based on CPU utilization.
4. **State Management**: Use Redis for caching product information and managing session states.

6.3 Implementation Steps

1. **Deploy Multiple Instances**: Use Kubernetes to deploy multiple replicas of each microservice.
2. **Configure Load Balancers**: Set up service types in Kubernetes to expose services externally.
3. **Implement HPA**: Configure Horizontal Pod Autoscaler to ensure services can scale up or down based on load.
4. **Monitor Performance**: Use Prometheus and Grafana to monitor the performance and health of services.

Conclusion

In this chapter, we explored the strategies and techniques for effectively scaling microservices, including:

- **Horizontal and vertical scaling** techniques to meet increasing demands.
- **Load balancing** strategies to distribute traffic across service instances.
- **Managing state** in microservices while maintaining scalability.

By implementing these practices, you can ensure that your microservices architecture can handle growing workloads, maintain performance, and remain resilient. In the next chapter, we will discuss security in microservices, covering authentication, authorization, and securing inter-service communication.

Chapter 9: Security in Microservices

As organizations increasingly adopt microservices architectures, the security of these distributed systems becomes paramount. Unlike monolithic applications, microservices communicate over networks, leading to unique security challenges. This chapter will explore the essential concepts of security in microservices, including authentication, authorization, secure communication, data protection, and best practices for ensuring robust security.

By the end of this chapter, you will have a comprehensive understanding of how to secure your microservices effectively and safeguard your applications against potential vulnerabilities and attacks.

Section 1: Understanding Security in Microservices

1.1 The Importance of Security in Microservices
Microservices architecture introduces various security challenges:

- **Increased Attack Surface**: Each microservice exposes its own APIs, increasing the number of potential entry points for attackers.
- **Service-to-Service Communication**: Microservices often need to communicate with each other, requiring secure authentication and authorization mechanisms.
- **Data Sensitivity**: Microservices may handle sensitive data that must be

protected both in transit and at rest.

1.2 Key Security Principles

To effectively secure microservices, organizations should adhere to several key principles:

- **Least Privilege**: Grant the minimum necessary permissions for users and services to perform their tasks. This limits potential damage from compromised accounts.
- **Defense in Depth**: Implement multiple layers of security measures to protect your microservices, making it more difficult for attackers to penetrate the system.
- **Secure by Design**: Incorporate security considerations into the design phase of microservices development rather than treating it as an afterthought.
- **Regular Security Audits**: Perform regular security audits and assessments to identify vulnerabilities and ensure compliance with security policies.

Section 2: Authentication in Microservices

2.1 What is Authentication?

Authentication is the process of verifying the identity of a user or service. In a microservices architecture, it is crucial to ensure that only legitimate users and services can access your microservices.

2.2 Common Authentication Methods

Several methods can be used for authentication in microservices:

- **Basic Authentication**: A simple method where the user provides a username and password encoded in the request header. While easy to implement, it should only be used over HTTPS due to security concerns.
- **Token-Based Authentication**: In this approach, the client receives a token after successful authentication, which is included in subsequent

requests. JSON Web Tokens (JWT) are commonly used for this purpose due to their compact size and ability to carry claims.

- **OAuth 2.0**: A widely used authorization framework that enables third-party applications to obtain limited access to user accounts on an HTTP service. OAuth 2.0 is often used in conjunction with OpenID Connect for user authentication.

2.3 Implementing Token-Based Authentication with JWT

Let's implement JWT authentication in our microservices using **ASP.NET Core**.

Step 1: Install Required Packages

Install the following NuGet package:

```bash
Copy code
dotnet add package Microsoft.
AspNetCore.Authentication.JwtBearer
```

Step 2: Configure JWT Authentication

In your Startup.cs (or Program.cs in .NET 6+), configure JWT authentication:

```csharp
Copy code
var builder = WebApplication.CreateBuilder(args);

// Configure JWT Authentication
builder.Services.AddAuthentication(options =>
{
    options.DefaultAuthenticateScheme =
    JwtBearerDefaults.AuthenticationScheme;
    options.DefaultChallengeScheme =
    JwtBearerDefaults.AuthenticationScheme;
})
.AddJwtBearer(options =>
{
```

```csharp
    options.TokenValidationParameters =
new TokenValidationParameters
    {
        ValidateIssuer = true,
        ValidateAudience = true,
        ValidateLifetime = true,
        ValidateIssuerSigningKey = true,
        ValidIssuer = builder.Configuration["Jwt:Issuer"],
        ValidAudience = builder.Configuration["Jwt:Audience"],
        IssuerSigningKey = new
SymmetricSecurityKey(Encoding.
UTF8.GetBytes(builder.
Configuration["Jwt:Key"]))
    };
});

builder.Services.AddControllers();

var app = builder.Build();
app.UseAuthentication();
app.UseAuthorization();
app.MapControllers();
app.Run();
```

Step 3: Generate JWT Tokens

Create an endpoint to authenticate users and generate JWT tokens:

```csharp
csharp
Copy code
[HttpPost("authenticate")]
public IActionResult Authenticate
([FromBody] UserLogin userLogin)
{
    // Validate user credentials (omitted for brevity)
    var tokenHandler = new JwtSecurityTokenHandler();
    var key = Encoding.ASCII.GetBytes(Configuration["Jwt:Key"]);
    var tokenDescriptor = new SecurityTokenDescriptor
    {
```

117

```
        Subject = new ClaimsIdentity(new[]
        {
            new Claim(ClaimTypes.Name, userLogin.Username)
        }),
        Expires = DateTime.UtcNow.AddHours(1),
        SigningCredentials = new SigningCredentials(new
        SymmetricSecurityKey(key),
   SecurityAlgorithms.
 HmacSha256Signature)
      };

      var token = tokenHandler.CreateToken(tokenDescriptor);
      return Ok(new { Token = tokenHandler.WriteToken(token) });
}
```

With this implementation, clients can authenticate and receive a JWT, which they will include in the Authorization header of subsequent requests:

```css
css
Copy code
Authorization: Bearer {token}
```

Section 3: Authorization in Microservices

3.1 What is Authorization?

Authorization determines what an authenticated user or service is allowed to do. It ensures that only authorized users can access specific resources or perform certain actions.

3.2 Common Authorization Mechanisms

Several mechanisms can be used for authorization in microservices:

- **Role-Based Access Control (RBAC)**: Users are assigned roles, and permissions are granted to those roles. This simplifies permission management.

- **Attribute-Based Access Control (ABAC)**: Access is granted based on attributes (user attributes, resource attributes, environment conditions) rather than roles.

3.3 Implementing Role-Based Authorization

You can implement role-based authorization in your microservices using the [Authorize] attribute.

1. **Define Roles in the User Model**:

Update your user model to include roles:

```csharp
Copy code
public class UserLogin
{
    public string Username { get; set; }
    public string Password { get; set; }
    public string Role { get; set; } // Add role property
}
```

1. **Authorize Roles in Controllers**:

Use the [Authorize] attribute to secure your endpoints:

```csharp
Copy code
[Authorize(Roles = "Admin")]
[HttpPost("create")]
public IActionResult CreateProduct(Product product)
{
    // Product creation logic
}
```

This example ensures that only users with the Admin role can access the

CreateProduct endpoint.

Section 4: Securing Communication Between Microservices

4.1 Importance of Securing Communication

As microservices often need to communicate with each other, securing inter-service communication is critical to protect sensitive data and prevent unauthorized access.

4.2 Transport Layer Security (TLS)

Transport Layer Security (TLS) is a cryptographic protocol designed to provide secure communication over a computer network. In microservices, TLS ensures that data in transit is encrypted and protected from eavesdropping.

Implementing HTTPS in ASP.NET Core

1. **Configure HTTPS**:

In your ASP.NET Core application, ensure that HTTPS is enabled by default. This can be done in launchSettings.json:

```json
Copy code
"profiles": {
    "IIS Express": {
        "commandName": "IISExpress",
        "launchBrowser": true,
        "environmentVariables": {
            "ASPNETCORE_ENVIRONMENT": "Development"
        }
    },
    "ProductService": {
        "commandName": "Project",
        "launchBrowser": true,
        "applicationUrl":
        "https://localhost:5001;http://localhost:5000",
```

```
    "environmentVariables": {
        "ASPNETCORE_ENVIRONMENT": "Development"
    }
  }
}
```

1. **Redirect HTTP to HTTPS**:

Add middleware to redirect HTTP requests to HTTPS in your Startup.cs or Program.cs:

```csharp
csharp
Copy code
app.UseHttpsRedirection();
```

4.3 Securing gRPC Communication

When using gRPC for communication between services, ensure that gRPC services are secured with TLS.

1. **Configure gRPC with SSL**:

In the appsettings.json, specify the server certificate:

```json
json
Copy code
"Kestrel": {
    "Certificates": {
        "Default": {
            "Path": "path/to/your/certificate.pfx",
            "Password": "your_certificate_password"
        }
    }
}
```

121

1. **Add gRPC Service with TLS**:

In your gRPC server configuration, ensure that you configure the gRPC server to require TLS:

```csharp
Copy code
var builder = WebApplication.CreateBuilder(args);
builder.WebHost.ConfigureKestrel(serverOptions =>
{
    serverOptions.ListenAnyIP(5001, listenOptions =>
    {
        listenOptions.UseHttps
("path/to/your/certificate.pfx",
"your_certificate_password");
    });
});
```

Section 5: Data Protection in Microservices

5.1 Protecting Sensitive Data

Microservices often handle sensitive information, making data protection critical. This includes ensuring that data is encrypted both at rest and in transit.

5.2 Encryption Strategies

1. **Encrypting Data at Rest**: Use encryption techniques to protect stored data. Most cloud providers offer encryption options for databases and storage solutions.
2. **Encrypting Data in Transit**: Ensure that all data transmitted between services is encrypted using TLS.
3. **Using Data Protection APIs**: ASP.NET Core provides Data Protection APIs for encrypting sensitive data such as connection strings, user data, and tokens.

Example: Using Data Protection in ASP.NET Core

1. **Install the Required Package**:

```bash
Copy code
dotnet add package Microsoft.AspNetCore.DataProtection
```

1. **Configure Data Protection in Startup.cs**:

```csharp
Copy code
services.AddDataProtection()
    .PersistKeysToFileSystem
(new DirectoryInfo(@"c:\keys"))
    .SetApplicationName("MyApp");
```

1. **Encrypt and Decrypt Data**:

```csharp
Copy code
var protector = dataProtectionProvider.
CreateProtector("MyPurpose");

// Encrypt data
string encryptedData = protector.Protect("SensitiveData");

// Decrypt data
string decryptedData = protector.Unprotect(encryptedData);
```

Section 6: Monitoring and Auditing Security

6.1 The Importance of Monitoring Security

Monitoring security is crucial for identifying potential threats, understanding system behavior, and ensuring compliance with security policies. Continuous monitoring helps organizations respond to security incidents proactively.

6.2 Implementing Security Monitoring

1. **Centralized Logging**: Aggregate logs from all microservices to a centralized logging solution such as the **ELK Stack** or **Splunk**. This allows for easier analysis and troubleshooting of security events.
2. **Security Information and Event Management (SIEM)**: Implement SIEM solutions to analyze security logs and detect suspicious activities. Tools like **Graylog**, **Splunk**, or **Azure Sentinel** can help identify potential threats in real-time.

6.3 Conducting Security Audits

Perform regular security audits to assess the effectiveness of your security measures. This includes:

- Reviewing access control policies.
- Conducting vulnerability assessments on your microservices.
- Ensuring compliance with industry regulations (e.g., GDPR, HIPAA).

Section 7: Case Study: Securing a Microservices Application

Let's walk through a case study of securing a microservices application that includes the **ProductService**, **OrderService**, and **NotificationService**.

7.1 Application Overview

- **ProductService**: Manages product information and exposes a RESTful API.

- **OrderService**: Processes orders and communicates with the **Product-Service** for product details.
- **NotificationService**: Sends notifications based on events published by the **ProductService**.

7.2 Security Architecture

1. **Authentication and Authorization**: Implement JWT-based authentication in the API Gateway to validate users and enforce authorization using RBAC.
2. **Secure Communication**: Use HTTPS for all services to encrypt data in transit, and implement mutual TLS for service-to-service communication.
3. **Data Protection**: Use ASP.NET Core Data Protection APIs to encrypt sensitive data stored in databases.

7.3 Implementation Steps

1. **Set Up JWT Authentication**: Configure JWT authentication in the API Gateway and validate tokens in each microservice.
2. **Enable HTTPS**: Configure each microservice to use HTTPS for secure communication.
3. **Implement Data Protection**: Use Data Protection APIs to encrypt sensitive data before storing it.

Conclusion

In this chapter, we explored the essential aspects of securing microservices, including:

- **Authentication and authorization** mechanisms to verify user identities and control access.
- **Securing communication** between services using TLS and best prac-

tices for data protection.

- **Monitoring and auditing** security to proactively identify threats and ensure compliance.

By implementing these security measures, you can protect your microservices architecture from vulnerabilities and attacks, ensuring the integrity and confidentiality of your applications and data. In the next chapter, we will delve into managing configurations in microservices, exploring techniques for centralized configuration management, versioning, and dynamic configuration updates.

Chapter 10: Managing Configurations in Microservices

I n a microservices architecture, managing configurations effectively is crucial for ensuring that services operate correctly across different environments. As microservices evolve and scale, the complexity of configuration management increases, making it essential to adopt strategies and tools that enable efficient and consistent configuration management. This chapter will explore various aspects of managing configurations in microservices, including centralized configuration management, versioning, dynamic configuration updates, environment-specific configurations, and best practices.

By the end of this chapter, you will have a comprehensive understanding of how to manage configurations effectively in your microservices architecture, ensuring consistency, reliability, and ease of deployment.

Section 1: The Importance of Configuration Management

1.1 Understanding Configuration Management

Configuration management involves managing and maintaining the settings and parameters of software applications, infrastructure, and services. In microservices, configuration management is critical because each service may have its own set of configuration requirements, leading to increased complexity.

1.2 Key Reasons for Configuration Management in Microservices

- **Consistency Across Environments**: Ensures that services behave the same way in development, testing, and production environments.
- **Simplified Deployment**: Streamlines the deployment process by managing configurations centrally, reducing the risk of configuration errors.
- **Easier Maintenance**: Allows for easy updates and changes to configurations without needing to modify code or redeploy services.

Section 2: Centralized Configuration Management

2.1 What is Centralized Configuration Management?

Centralized configuration management involves storing configuration settings in a single location, allowing all microservices to access them. This approach simplifies management and reduces the risk of discrepancies between configurations in different environments.

2.2 Benefits of Centralized Configuration Management

- **Single Source of Truth**: Centralized management provides a consistent view of configurations across all services, reducing the likelihood of misconfigurations.
- **Ease of Updates**: Configurations can be updated in one place, automatically propagating changes to all services that rely on them.
- **Improved Security**: Centralized management allows for better control over sensitive configurations, such as API keys and connection strings.

2.3 Implementing Centralized Configuration Management with Spring Cloud Config

Spring Cloud Config is a popular solution for managing configurations in microservices. Although primarily designed for Java applications, its principles can be applied in various environments.

Step 1: Set Up Spring Cloud Config Server

1. **Create a Spring Boot Project**: Use Spring Initializr to create a new Spring Boot project with the Spring Cloud Config Server dependency.
2. **Add Configuration**: In application.yml, configure the config server:

```yaml
Copy code
server:
  port: 8888

spring:
  cloud:
    config:
      server:
        git:
          uri: https://github.com/your-repo/config-repo
```

1. **Run the Config Server**: Start the Spring Cloud Config server. It will fetch configuration files from the specified Git repository.

Step 2: Accessing Configurations in Microservices

1. **Add Dependencies**: In your microservice projects, include the Spring Cloud Starter Config dependency.
2. **Configure the Microservice**: In application.yml, specify the config server URL:

```yaml
Copy code
spring:
  application:
```

```
    name: productservice
 cloud:
   config:
     uri: http://localhost:8888
```

1. **Access Configurations**: The microservice can now access configurations stored in the config server using the /productservice endpoint.

Section 3: Versioning Configurations

3.1 Why Version Configurations?

As microservices evolve, configurations may change over time. **Versioning configurations** helps track changes, rollback if necessary, and manage different versions of configurations for different environments or service instances.

3.2 Implementing Configuration Versioning

When using a centralized configuration management tool, versioning is typically built-in. For instance, in Spring Cloud Config, you can manage versions of configuration files stored in a Git repository. Each commit to the repository represents a version of the configuration.

1. **Branching Strategy**: Use Git branching strategies (e.g., feature branches, release branches) to manage different versions of configurations.
2. **Tagging Releases**: Tag stable releases of configurations to easily identify and roll back to specific versions if needed.

Section 4: Dynamic Configuration Updates

4.1 What are Dynamic Configuration Updates?

Dynamic configuration updates allow microservices to adapt to configuration changes without requiring redeployment. This is particularly useful for adjusting settings based on runtime conditions, such as scaling up resources during peak load.

4.2 Implementing Dynamic Configuration Updates

1. **Spring Cloud Config with Refresh Scope**: If using Spring Cloud Config, you can enable refreshable configurations. Annotate your beans with @RefreshScope, allowing them to refresh their configuration when changes occur.

```java
Copy code
@RefreshScope
@Service
public class ProductService {
    @Value("${product.default.price}")
    private double defaultPrice;
}
```

1. **Using a REST Endpoint**: Expose an endpoint in your microservice to trigger a refresh:

```java
Copy code
@PostMapping("/refresh")
public ResponseEntity<Void> refresh() {
    context.publishEvent(new RefreshScopeRefreshedEvent(this));
    return ResponseEntity.ok().build();
}
```

1. **Event-Driven Updates**: Implement an event-driven architecture where services listen for configuration change events, allowing them to update their settings dynamically.

Section 5: Environment-Specific Configurations

5.1 Managing Environment-Specific Configurations

Microservices typically run in multiple environments (development, testing, production), each with its own configuration needs. Managing environment-specific configurations effectively is crucial for smooth operations.

5.2 Techniques for Managing Environment-Specific Configurations

1. **Environment Variables**: Use environment variables to define environment-specific configurations. This approach allows you to set different values for each environment without modifying code.
2. **Profiles**: If using Spring Boot, leverage profiles to create environment-specific configuration files (e.g., application-dev.yml, application-prod.yml). Specify the active profile in your configuration:

```yaml
Copy code
spring:
  profiles:
    active: dev
```

1. **Configuration Management Tools**: Use tools like **HashiCorp Consul** or **Spring Cloud Config** to manage environment-specific configurations centrally.

Section 6: Best Practices for Configuration Management

6.1 Adopt Infrastructure as Code (IaC)

Implement Infrastructure as Code practices to manage your infrastructure and configurations programmatically. Use tools like **Terraform**, **Ansible**, or **Azure Resource Manager** to define and provision your infrastructure.

6.2 Use Configuration Management Tools

Utilize configuration management tools to automate and manage configurations across environments. Popular tools include:

- **Spring Cloud Config**: For centralized configuration management.
- **Consul**: For service discovery and configuration management.
- **Etcd**: A distributed key-value store for managing configuration data.

6.3 Secure Sensitive Data

Ensure that sensitive configuration data (e.g., API keys, database connection strings) is stored securely. Use encryption and access controls to protect sensitive information.

6.4 Version Control for Configuration Files

Store configuration files in a version control system (e.g., Git) to track changes, enable collaboration, and facilitate rollback when necessary.

Section 7: Case Study: Managing Configurations in a Microservices Application

Let's explore a case study of managing configurations in a microservices application that includes the **ProductService, OrderService**, and **NotificationService**.

7.1 Application Overview

- **ProductService**: Manages product information and exposes a RESTful API.
- **OrderService**: Processes orders and communicates with the **ProductService** for product details.
- **NotificationService**: Sends notifications based on events published by the **ProductService**.

7.2 Configuration Management Strategy

1. **Centralized Configuration**: Use Spring Cloud Config to manage configurations centrally for all services.
2. **Version Control**: Store configuration files in a Git repository, allowing for versioning and tracking changes.
3. **Dynamic Updates**: Implement refreshable configurations to allow services to update their settings without redeployment.
4. **Environment-Specific Configurations**: Use profiles to manage environment-specific settings for each microservice.

7.3 Implementation Steps

1. **Set Up Spring Cloud Config**: Create a Spring Cloud Config server to manage configurations centrally.
2. **Store Configurations in Git**: Store configuration files in a Git repository, organizing them by service and environment.
3. **Implement Dynamic Configuration Updates**: Enable refreshable configurations and expose an endpoint to trigger updates.
4. **Test Configurations Across Environments**: Validate configurations in development and staging environments before promoting them to production.

Conclusion

In this chapter, we explored the critical aspects of managing configurations in microservices, including:

- **Centralized configuration management** to streamline configuration processes.
- **Versioning configurations** to track changes and facilitate rollbacks.
- **Dynamic configuration updates** to allow services to adapt to changing conditions without redeployment.
- **Environment-specific configurations** to manage settings for different environments effectively.

By implementing these practices, you can ensure that your microservices are configured consistently and effectively, reducing complexity and improving deployment reliability. In the next chapter, we will explore strategies for handling data consistency and transactions in microservices, including patterns like Saga and CQRS, as well as techniques for managing distributed transactions.

Chapter 11: Data Consistency and Transactions in Microservices

As organizations transition to microservices architectures, ensuring data consistency and managing transactions across distributed services becomes a significant challenge. Unlike monolithic applications, where transactions can span a single database, microservices often rely on multiple independent data stores, leading to complexity in maintaining data integrity. This chapter explores the intricacies of data consistency in microservices, the challenges posed by distributed transactions, and effective patterns for managing data integrity.

By the end of this chapter, you will have a comprehensive understanding of how to handle data consistency and transactions in your microservices architecture, leveraging patterns like the Saga and CQRS to ensure reliability and integrity.

Section 1: Understanding Data Consistency in Microservices

1.1 The Importance of Data Consistency

Data consistency refers to the property of a database where data is in a valid state and conforms to defined rules. In microservices, maintaining data consistency is crucial to ensure that the system behaves as expected and that users receive accurate information.

1.2 Types of Data Consistency

There are several models of data consistency:

- **Strong Consistency**: Guarantees that any read operation reflects the most recent write. This model is typically challenging to achieve in distributed systems.
- **Eventual Consistency**: Allows for temporary inconsistencies, with the guarantee that, given enough time, all updates will propagate to all nodes, and all replicas will converge to the same value. This model is more achievable in distributed systems and is often used in microservices.
- **Causal Consistency**: Ensures that operations that are causally related are seen by all nodes in the same order. This model is useful in scenarios where the order of operations matters.

Section 2: Challenges of Distributed Transactions

2.1 The Complexity of Distributed Transactions

In a microservices architecture, a single transaction may need to involve multiple services, each with its own database. This leads to several challenges:

- **Network Latency**: Communication between services over a network can introduce latency, complicating transaction management.
- **Partial Failures**: One service may succeed while another fails, leaving the system in an inconsistent state.
- **Lack of Atomicity**: Traditional databases provide atomic transactions, but in a distributed system, ensuring atomicity across multiple services is complex.

2.2 The Two-Phase Commit Protocol

The **Two-Phase Commit (2PC)** protocol is a classic solution for managing distributed transactions. It involves a coordinator that orchestrates the transaction across multiple participants:

1. **Prepare Phase**: The coordinator sends a prepare request to all participants. Each participant votes on whether they can commit the transaction based on their local state.
2. **Commit Phase**: If all participants vote to commit, the coordinator sends a commit request. If any participant votes to abort, the coordinator sends an abort request to all participants.

While 2PC ensures atomicity, it can lead to blocking and increased latency, making it less suitable for microservices architectures.

Section 3: The Saga Pattern

3.1 What is the Saga Pattern?

The **Saga pattern** is an alternative to 2PC for managing distributed transactions in microservices. Instead of a single coordinator, a Saga consists of a series of local transactions, each managed by individual services. Each local transaction updates its data and publishes an event or message to trigger the next transaction.

3.2 Types of Sagas

There are two primary types of Sagas:

- **Choreography-Based Saga**: Each service involved in the Saga listens for events and triggers the next step in the process. This approach reduces coupling but can be complex to manage.
- **Orchestration-Based Saga**: A central orchestrator manages the flow of the Saga, directing each service on when to execute its local transaction. This approach simplifies the flow but introduces a single point of failure.

3.3 Implementing the Saga Pattern

Let's implement a Saga pattern using an orchestration-based approach for a **OrderService** and **PaymentService**.

Step 1: Define the Saga Steps

1. **Order Creation**: The **OrderService** creates an order.
2. **Payment Processing**: The **PaymentService** processes the payment.
3. **Order Confirmation**: Upon successful payment, the **OrderService** confirms the order.

Step 2: Implement the Orchestrator

Create an orchestrator service that manages the Saga:

```csharp
Copy code
public class OrderOrchestrator
{
    private readonly IOrderService _orderService;
    private readonly IPaymentService _paymentService;

    public OrderOrchestrator(IOrderService orderService,
    IPaymentService paymentService)
    {
        _orderService = orderService;
        _paymentService = paymentService;
    }

    public async Task<bool> ProcessOrder(Order order)
    {
        // Step 1: Create the order
        var createdOrder = await _orderService.CreateOrder(order);

        if (createdOrder == null)
            return false;

        // Step 2: Process payment
        var paymentSuccess = await
        _paymentService.ProcessPayment(createdOrder.Id,
        order.PaymentDetails);

        if (!paymentSuccess)
        {
            // Step 3: Rollback order creation if payment fails
```

```
        await _orderService.CancelOrder(createdOrder.Id);
        return false;
    }

    // Step 4: Confirm the order if payment is successful
    await _orderService.ConfirmOrder(createdOrder.Id);
    return true;
    }
}
```

In this example, the orchestrator manages the flow of the Saga and handles any rollback operations if a step fails.

Section 4: Command Query Responsibility Segregation (CQRS)

4.1 What is CQRS?

Command Query Responsibility Segregation (CQRS) is a pattern that separates the responsibility of handling commands (writes) from queries (reads). This separation allows for optimized data storage and access patterns.

4.2 Benefits of CQRS

- **Scalability**: Allows for independent scaling of read and write operations, optimizing performance based on specific workload characteristics.
- **Simplified Models**: By separating concerns, the codebase can be simplified, making it easier to manage.
- **Improved Performance**: Queries can be optimized for read operations, and commands can be designed for write operations, improving overall system performance.

4.3 Implementing CQRS in Microservices

To implement CQRS in a microservices architecture, consider the following steps:

Step 1: Define the Command and Query Models

1. **Command Model**: Define the data model and operations for write operations (e.g., creating or updating an order).

```csharp
Copy code
public class CreateOrderCommand
{
    public string ProductId { get; set; }
    public int Quantity { get; set; }
    public string CustomerId { get; set; }
}
```

1. **Query Model**: Define the data model and operations for read operations.

```csharp
Copy code
public class OrderQueryModel
{
    public string OrderId { get; set; }
    public string ProductId { get; set; }
    public int Quantity { get; set; }
    public string CustomerId { get; set; }
    public string Status { get; set; }
}
```

Step 2: Implement Command and Query Handlers

Create separate handlers for commands and queries.

1. **Command Handler**:

```csharp
csharp
Copy code
public class OrderCommandHandler
{
    private readonly IOrderRepository _orderRepository;

    public OrderCommandHandler(IOrderRepository orderRepository)
    {
        _orderRepository = orderRepository;
    }

    public async Task Handle(CreateOrderCommand command)
    {
        // Implement order creation logic
        var order = new Order { ProductId = command.ProductId,
        Quantity = command.Quantity, Status = "Pending" };
        await _orderRepository.AddOrderAsync(order);
    }
}
```

1. **Query Handler**:

```csharp
csharp
Copy code
public class OrderQueryHandler
{
    private readonly IOrderReadRepository _orderReadRepository;

    public OrderQueryHandler(IOrderReadRepository
    orderReadRepository)
    {
        _orderReadRepository = orderReadRepository;
    }

    public async Task<OrderQueryModel> Handle(string orderId)
    {
```

```csharp
    var order = await
    _orderReadRepository.GetOrderByIdAsync(orderId);
    return new OrderQueryModel
    {
        OrderId = order.Id,
        ProductId = order.ProductId,
        Quantity = order.Quantity,
        CustomerId = order.CustomerId,
        Status = order.Status
    };
    }
}
```

Section 5: Data Consistency Techniques

5.1 Eventual Consistency

Eventual consistency is a model used in distributed systems to ensure that, given enough time, all replicas of a piece of data will converge to the same value. While immediate consistency is often impractical in microservices, eventual consistency provides a practical approach to data integrity.

Implementing Eventual Consistency

1. **Publish Events**: When a service updates its state, it can publish an event to notify other services.

```csharp
csharp
Copy code
public class OrderService
{
    private readonly IEventPublisher _eventPublisher;

    public OrderService(IEventPublisher eventPublisher)
```

```
    {
        _eventPublisher = eventPublisher;
    }

    public async Task CreateOrder(Order order)
    {
        // Save order logic
        await _eventPublisher.PublishAsync(new
        OrderCreatedEvent(order.Id));
    }
}
```

1. **Subscribe to Events**: Other services can subscribe to events and update their state accordingly.

```csharp
Copy code
public class InventoryService
{
    public void OnOrderCreated(OrderCreatedEvent orderEvent)
    {
        // Update inventory based on the order
    }
}
```

5.2 Two-Phase Commit Alternatives

While the Two-Phase Commit protocol ensures atomicity across services, it is often impractical for microservices. Alternatives to 2PC include:

- **Compensating Transactions**: Instead of rolling back, you create compensating actions to undo the effects of a previous transaction.
- **Saga Pattern**: As discussed earlier, the Saga pattern allows for handling distributed transactions with multiple local transactions and compensating actions.

Section 6: Monitoring Data Consistency

6.1 The Importance of Monitoring

Monitoring data consistency in microservices is essential for identifying issues and ensuring that services remain in sync. By implementing monitoring strategies, you can detect anomalies and respond proactively to potential issues.

6.2 Techniques for Monitoring Data Consistency

1. **Audit Logging**: Implement audit logging to track changes made to data across services. This can help identify inconsistencies and trace the flow of data.

2. **Data Validation**: Periodically validate data across services to ensure consistency. This can be done using background jobs that compare data between services.

3. **Alerts and Notifications**: Set up alerts to notify teams of potential data inconsistencies, such as discrepancies in order statuses across services.

Section 7: Case Study: Managing Data Consistency in a Microservices Application

Let's explore a case study of managing data consistency in a microservices application that includes the **ProductService**, **OrderService**, and **NotificationService**.

7.1 Application Overview

- **ProductService**: Manages product information.
- **OrderService**: Processes orders and communicates with the **ProductService** for product details.
- **NotificationService**: Sends notifications based on events published by the **OrderService**.

7.2 Data Consistency Strategy

1. **Implement the Saga Pattern**: Use the Saga pattern to manage transactions across services, ensuring that each service can handle its own local transactions and notify others as needed.
2. **Eventual Consistency**: Adopt an eventual consistency model, where services respond to events and update their state over time.
3. **CQRS for Data Management**: Implement CQRS to separate command and query responsibilities, optimizing performance and scalability.

7.3 Implementation Steps

1. **Define Sagas for Order Processing**: Implement the Saga pattern in the OrderService to manage the order creation process, triggering events for other services.
2. **Use Event Sourcing**: Store events representing changes in the state of orders to allow for auditing and reconstructing states as needed.
3. **Set Up Monitoring**: Implement monitoring strategies to track data consistency and detect anomalies.

Conclusion

In this chapter, we explored the critical aspects of managing data consistency and transactions in microservices, including:

- The challenges of distributed transactions and the limitations of traditional methods like Two-Phase Commit.
- The Saga pattern and CQRS as effective strategies for managing data consistency.
- Techniques for monitoring data consistency and ensuring the integrity of microservices.

By adopting these practices, you can maintain data integrity and consistency in your microservices architecture, enabling your applications to scale and evolve effectively. In the next chapter, we will delve into best practices for deploying microservices in production environments, focusing on strategies for reliability, scaling, and monitoring in cloud-native architectures.

Chapter 12: Best Practices for Deploying Microservices in Production

Deploying microservices into production requires careful planning, robust strategies, and a solid understanding of the challenges involved. Unlike traditional monolithic applications, microservices architecture introduces complexities in deployment, configuration, and management. This chapter explores best practices for deploying microservices in production, ensuring reliability, scalability, and security.

By the end of this chapter, you will have a comprehensive understanding of the best practices for deploying microservices effectively, enabling you to build resilient and efficient applications.

Section 1: Preparing for Deployment

1.1 Assessing Application Readiness

Before deploying microservices into production, it is essential to assess their readiness. Consider the following aspects:

- **Functionality**: Ensure that all features work as expected and that the application meets the defined requirements.
- **Performance**: Conduct load testing to validate the performance of your microservices under expected traffic conditions.

- **Security**: Perform security assessments to identify and remediate vulnerabilities.

1.2 Establishing Deployment Criteria
Define clear criteria for deployment, including:

- **Code Quality**: Ensure that code passes automated tests and adheres to coding standards.
- **Documentation**: Maintain up-to-date documentation, including architecture diagrams, API specifications, and deployment instructions.
- **Backup and Rollback Plans**: Prepare backup solutions and rollback strategies in case of deployment failures.

Section 2: CI/CD Pipelines for Microservices

2.1 What is CI/CD?
Continuous Integration (CI) and **Continuous Deployment (CD)** are essential practices for modern software development, allowing teams to automate the process of integrating code changes, running tests, and deploying applications.
2.2 Benefits of CI/CD in Microservices

- **Faster Delivery**: CI/CD enables quicker release cycles, allowing teams to deliver features and fixes rapidly.
- **Consistent Quality**: Automated testing ensures that new changes do not introduce bugs or regressions.
- **Reduced Deployment Risk**: Smaller, incremental updates reduce the risk of deployment failures compared to large releases.

2.3 Implementing CI/CD Pipelines
To implement CI/CD for microservices, follow these steps:
Step 1: Set Up a Version Control System
Use a version control system (e.g., Git) to manage your microservices

codebase. Organize your repositories by service to facilitate independent development and deployment.

Step 2: Automate Builds and Tests

Create a CI pipeline to automate the build and testing process:

1. **Use CI Tools**: Tools like **Jenkins, GitHub Actions, CircleCI,** or **GitLab CI** can automate builds and tests.
2. **Define a CI Pipeline**: Configure a CI pipeline to build your microservices and run unit tests upon every code change.

Example: GitHub Actions CI Pipeline

```yaml
yaml
Copy code
name: CI Pipeline

on:
  push:
    branches:
      - main

jobs:
  build:
    runs-on: ubuntu-latest
    steps:
      - name: Checkout Code
        uses: actions/checkout@v2

      - name: Set Up .NET
        uses: actions/setup-dotnet@v1
        with:
          dotnet-version: '8.0.x'

      - name: Restore Dependencies
        run: dotnet restore

      - name: Build
```

```
    run: dotnet build --configuration Release --no-restore

  - name: Run Tests
    run: dotnet test --no-build --verbosity normal
```

Step 3: Automate Deployment

Create a CD pipeline to deploy your microservices automatically:

1. **Deploy to Staging**: Automatically deploy code changes to a staging environment for further testing.
2. **Promote to Production**: Once validated, promote the changes to the production environment.

Example: GitHub Actions CD Pipeline

```yaml
yaml
Copy code
name: CD Pipeline

on:
  push:
    branches:
      - main

jobs:
  deploy:
    runs-on: ubuntu-latest
    steps:
      - name: Checkout Code
        uses: actions/checkout@v2

      - name: Build Docker Image
        run: |
          docker build . -t
          your-dockerhub-username/productservice:latest
          echo "${{ secrets.DOCKER_PASSWORD }}" | docker login -u
```

```
    "${{ secrets.DOCKER_USERNAME }}" --password-stdin
    docker push
    your-dockerhub-username/productservice:latest

 - name: Deploy to Kubernetes
   run: |
       kubectl set image deployment/productservice
       productservice=your-dockerhub-username/productservice:latest
```

Section 3: Monitoring Microservices in Production

3.1 The Importance of Monitoring

Monitoring is critical for ensuring the health and performance of microservices in production. Effective monitoring provides visibility into application behavior, allowing teams to detect and respond to issues proactively.

3.2 Key Metrics to Monitor

Identify key metrics to monitor in your microservices, including:

- **Response Time**: Time taken to process requests.
- **Error Rate**: Percentage of failed requests compared to total requests.
- **Throughput**: Number of requests processed in a given time period.
- **Resource Utilization**: CPU, memory, and disk usage of services.

3.3 Implementing Monitoring Solutions

1. **Centralized Logging**: Aggregate logs from all microservices to a centralized logging solution (e.g., ELK Stack, Splunk) for easy analysis and troubleshooting.
2. **Monitoring Tools**: Use monitoring tools such as **Prometheus** and **Grafana** to track metrics and visualize performance data.

Example: Setting Up Prometheus and Grafana

- **Install Prometheus**: Set up Prometheus to scrape metrics from your microservices.

```yaml
Copy code
global:
  scrape_interval: 15s

scrape_configs:
  - job_name: 'productservice'
    static_configs:
      - targets: ['productservice:5000']
```

- **Install Grafana**: Use Grafana to create dashboards for visualizing metrics collected by Prometheus.

Section 4: Ensuring Resilience in Microservices

4.1 Understanding Resilience

Resilience refers to the ability of an application to handle failures and recover quickly. In microservices, resilience is crucial due to the distributed nature of services and the potential for individual service failures.

4.2 Implementing Resilience Patterns

1. **Circuit Breaker Pattern**: This pattern prevents a service from making requests to a failing service. When a service detects repeated failures, it opens the circuit and temporarily blocks requests until the service recovers.
2. **Retry Pattern**: Implement retry logic to automatically retry failed requests a specified number of times before considering the operation a failure.
3. **Fallback Pattern**: Provide a fallback mechanism that returns a default response or an alternative action when a service fails.

Example: Implementing Circuit Breaker with Polly

Install the **Polly** package:

```bash
Copy code
dotnet add package Polly
```

Use Polly to implement a circuit breaker in your service:

```csharp
Copy code
var policy = Policy
    .Handle<HttpRequestException>()
    .CircuitBreaker(2, TimeSpan.FromMinutes(1));

await policy.ExecuteAsync(() =>
_httpClient.GetAsync("https://example.com/api"));
```

Section 5: Scaling Microservices in Production

5.1 The Need for Scaling

As applications grow, scaling becomes essential to handle increased load and maintain performance. Scaling can be achieved through horizontal scaling (adding more instances) or vertical scaling (increasing resources on existing instances).

5.2 Strategies for Scaling Microservices

1. **Horizontal Scaling**: Deploy multiple instances of your microservices behind a load balancer. Use orchestration tools like Kubernetes to manage scaling.

2. **Auto-Scaling**: Implement auto-scaling based on metrics such as CPU usage or request latency. Kubernetes Horizontal Pod Autoscaler (HPA) can automatically adjust the number of pods based on defined metrics.

Example: Configuring HPA in Kubernetes

```yaml
yaml
Copy code
apiVersion: autoscaling/v2beta2
kind: HorizontalPodAutoscaler
metadata:
  name: productservice-hpa
spec:
  scaleTargetRef:
    apiVersion: apps/v1
    kind: Deployment
    name: productservice
  minReplicas: 3
  maxReplicas: 10
  metrics:
    - type: Resource
      resource:
        name: cpu
        target:
          type: Utilization
          averageUtilization: 50
```

Section 6: Securing Microservices in Production

6.1 The Importance of Security

Security is a critical aspect of deploying microservices in production. With multiple services communicating over networks, it is essential to implement robust security measures to protect sensitive data and ensure that only authorized users can access services.

6.2 Security Best Practices

1. **Use HTTPS**: Ensure that all services communicate over HTTPS to encrypt data in transit.
2. **Implement Authentication and Authorization**: Use token-based authentication (e.g., JWT) to secure APIs, and enforce authorization

rules to control access.

3. **Validate Input**: Implement input validation to protect against injection attacks and other vulnerabilities.

4. **Regularly Update Dependencies**: Keep your microservices and their dependencies up to date to mitigate vulnerabilities.

5. **Conduct Security Audits**: Perform regular security audits and penetration testing to identify and address potential weaknesses.

Section 7: Case Study: Deploying Microservices in Production

Let's walk through a case study of deploying a microservices application that includes the **ProductService**, **OrderService**, and **NotificationService** into production.

7.1 Application Overview

- **ProductService**: Manages product information and exposes a RESTful API.
- **OrderService**: Processes orders and communicates with the **ProductService** for product details.
- **NotificationService**: Sends notifications based on events published by the **OrderService**.

7.2 Deployment Strategy

1. **Set Up CI/CD Pipelines**: Implement CI/CD pipelines for automated testing and deployment of microservices.

2. **Use Kubernetes for Orchestration**: Deploy microservices to a Kubernetes cluster, enabling easy scaling and management.

3. **Monitor Performance**: Use Prometheus and Grafana to monitor the performance of microservices in production.

4. **Implement Resilience Patterns**: Apply circuit breaker and retry patterns to enhance the resilience of services.

5. **Secure Communication**: Ensure that all communications between

services are secured using HTTPS and authentication mechanisms.

7.3 Implementation Steps

1. **Create CI/CD Pipelines**: Set up pipelines for building, testing, and deploying microservices automatically.
2. **Deploy to Kubernetes**: Use Helm charts or Kubernetes manifests to deploy services into the cluster.
3. **Configure Monitoring**: Set up Prometheus and Grafana to visualize metrics and monitor the health of microservices.
4. **Test and Validate**: Conduct thorough testing in staging environments before promoting changes to production.

Conclusion

In this chapter, we explored the best practices for deploying microservices in production, including:

- The importance of preparation, CI/CD pipelines, and automated testing.
- Strategies for monitoring and ensuring resilience in microservices.
- Techniques for scaling and securing microservices effectively.

By adopting these best practices, you can ensure that your microservices are deployed reliably, efficiently, and securely in production environments. In the next chapter, we will discuss managing the lifecycle of microservices, focusing on versioning, deprecation, and retirement of services as applications evolve.

Chapter 13: Managing the Lifecycle of Microservices

As microservices architectures evolve, managing the lifecycle of individual services becomes essential for maintaining application quality, minimizing downtime, and ensuring that services meet business needs. Each microservice has its own lifecycle, including phases such as development, deployment, operation, versioning, deprecation, and retirement. This chapter will explore best practices and strategies for managing the lifecycle of microservices effectively.

By the end of this chapter, you will have a comprehensive understanding of how to manage the lifecycle of your microservices, including versioning strategies, handling deprecation, and planning for retirement.

Section 1: Understanding the Microservices Lifecycle

1.1 The Phases of a Microservices Lifecycle

The lifecycle of a microservice typically includes the following phases:

1. **Development**: The phase where the microservice is designed, implemented, and tested.
2. **Deployment**: The process of releasing the microservice to production environments.

3. **Operation**: The ongoing use and monitoring of the microservice in production.
4. **Versioning**: Managing changes and updates to the microservice over time.
5. **Deprecation**: The process of phasing out a microservice in favor of newer versions or alternative services.
6. **Retirement**: The final phase where the microservice is removed from production.

1.2 Importance of Lifecycle Management
Effective lifecycle management is crucial for several reasons:

- **Consistency**: Ensures that all services are maintained and updated consistently across environments.
- **Quality**: Helps maintain high-quality standards throughout the service's lifecycle.
- **Business Continuity**: Reduces the risk of downtime and disruptions as services are updated or replaced.
- **Adaptability**: Allows organizations to adapt to changing business requirements and technologies.

Section 2: Development Phase

2.1 Best Practices for Development
During the development phase, consider the following best practices:

- **Microservices Design Principles**: Follow principles such as single responsibility, decoupling, and API-first design to ensure services are well-architected.
- **Automated Testing**: Implement automated unit, integration, and end-to-end tests to ensure service functionality and reliability.
- **Documentation**: Maintain comprehensive documentation for APIs, architecture, and deployment processes to facilitate collaboration and

onboarding.

2.2 Tools for Development

Utilize development tools that enhance productivity and collaboration:

- **Version Control Systems**: Use Git for managing source code and collaborating with team members.
- **Integrated Development Environments (IDEs)**: Choose IDEs like Visual Studio, IntelliJ IDEA, or VS Code that support microservices development with relevant plugins and tools.
- **CI/CD Tools**: Implement CI/CD tools (e.g., Jenkins, GitHub Actions, GitLab CI) to automate the build, testing, and deployment processes.

Section 3: Deployment Phase

3.1 Deployment Strategies

Choosing the right deployment strategy is crucial for minimizing downtime and ensuring a smooth rollout. Consider the following strategies:

- **Blue-Green Deployment**: Maintain two identical environments (blue and green). Route traffic to the new version (green) while keeping the current version (blue) active for fallback.
- **Canary Releases**: Gradually roll out the new version to a small subset of users before deploying it to the entire user base. This approach allows for testing in production and monitoring for issues.
- **Rolling Updates**: Update instances of the service gradually, replacing old instances with new ones. This approach ensures that some instances are always available to handle traffic.

3.2 Implementing Deployment Strategies

Example: Implementing Blue-Green Deployment

1. **Prepare Environments**: Create two identical environments for the

application (blue and green).

2. **Deploy New Version**: Deploy the new version of the service to the green environment.

3. **Switch Traffic**: Update the load balancer to route traffic from the blue environment to the green environment.

4. **Monitor Performance**: Monitor the green environment for issues. If problems occur, revert traffic back to the blue environment.

Section 4: Operation Phase

4.1 Monitoring Microservices in Production

Effective monitoring is essential for maintaining service health and performance. Key areas to monitor include:

- **Service Metrics**: Track metrics such as response times, error rates, and resource utilization to identify performance bottlenecks.
- **Logs**: Centralize logs from all microservices to facilitate troubleshooting and analysis.
- **Alerts**: Set up alerting mechanisms to notify teams of potential issues before they impact users.

4.2 Tools for Monitoring

Utilize monitoring tools and platforms to gain insights into microservice performance:

- **Prometheus**: An open-source monitoring and alerting toolkit that collects metrics from configured services.
- **Grafana**: A visualization tool that works with Prometheus to create dashboards for monitoring service health.
- **ELK Stack**: A combination of Elasticsearch, Logstash, and Kibana for centralized logging and log analysis.

Section 5: Versioning Microservices

5.1 The Importance of Versioning

As microservices evolve, versioning is essential to manage changes without disrupting existing functionality. Proper versioning allows teams to introduce new features while maintaining compatibility with older versions.

5.2 Versioning Strategies

1. **URI Versioning**: Include the version number in the API endpoint URL (e.g., /api/v1/products). This approach is straightforward and easily understood by consumers.
2. **Header Versioning**: Use HTTP headers to specify the version of the API being requested. This approach keeps URLs clean and allows for more flexible version management.
3. **Media Type Versioning**: Utilize custom media types in the Accept header to indicate the desired version of the API (e.g., application/vnd. example.v1+json).

5.3 Implementing Versioning

Example: URI Versioning in ASP.NET Core

1. Define versioned controllers in your ASP.NET Core application:

```csharp
Copy code
[ApiController]
[Route("api/v1/[controller]")]
public class ProductsV1Controller : ControllerBase
{
    // GET api/v1/products
    [HttpGet]
    public IActionResult GetProducts() { ... }
}
```

```
[ApiController]
[Route("api/v2/[controller]")]
public class ProductsV2Controller : ControllerBase
{
    // GET api/v2/products
    [HttpGet]
    public IActionResult GetProducts() { ... }
}
```

1. Update your routing configuration to support versioned APIs.

Section 6: Deprecation of Microservices

6.1 Understanding Deprecation

Deprecation is the process of phasing out a microservice or a version of an API while providing a clear path for users to transition to newer versions. Proper management of deprecation minimizes disruption and allows users to adapt to changes.

6.2 Best Practices for Deprecation

1. **Communicate Changes**: Inform users well in advance about the deprecation of services or API versions. Provide documentation and migration guides to assist in the transition.
2. **Support Legacy Versions**: Maintain support for deprecated versions for a specified period, allowing users to transition smoothly.
3. **Use Warning Headers**: Include warning headers in API responses to notify users about upcoming deprecation.

Example: Adding Warning Headers in ASP.NET Core

```csharp
csharp
Copy code
[HttpGet]
public IActionResult GetProducts()
{
    Response.Headers.Add("Warning", "299 - 'This API version is
    deprecated and will be removed on YYYY-MM-DD'");
    return Ok(products);
}
```

Section 7: Retirement of Microservices

7.1 The Retirement Process

Retirement is the final phase of a microservice's lifecycle, where it is removed from production and no longer maintained. Planning for retirement is essential to ensure a smooth transition and minimize disruption.

7.2 Steps for Retiring a Microservice

1. **Assess Impact**: Evaluate the impact of retiring the service on users and other dependent services.
2. **Communicate with Stakeholders**: Notify users and stakeholders of the retirement plan, including timelines and migration paths.
3. **Migrate Dependencies**: Ensure that any dependencies on the service are migrated to new versions or alternatives.
4. **Remove the Service**: Once all dependencies are handled, remove the service from production and decommission any related infrastructure.

Section 8: Case Study: Managing the Lifecycle of a Microservices Application

Let's walk through a case study of managing the lifecycle of a microservices application that includes the **ProductService**, **OrderService**, and **NotificationService**.

8.1 Application Overview

- **ProductService**: Manages product information and exposes a RESTful API.
- **OrderService**: Processes orders and communicates with the **ProductService** for product details.
- **NotificationService**: Sends notifications based on events published by the **OrderService**.

8.2 Lifecycle Management Strategy

1. **Development Phase**: Follow best practices for design, automated testing, and documentation to ensure high-quality microservices.
2. **Deployment Phase**: Implement CI/CD pipelines to automate the build, testing, and deployment processes.
3. **Operation Phase**: Monitor service performance and health using Prometheus and Grafana, implementing resilience patterns as needed.
4. **Versioning**: Use URI versioning to manage changes and ensure backward compatibility.
5. **Deprecation and Retirement**: Plan and communicate deprecation and retirement processes, ensuring a smooth transition for users.

8.3 Implementation Steps

1. **Set Up CI/CD Pipelines**: Create CI/CD pipelines for automated testing and deployment of each microservice.
2. **Implement Monitoring**: Set up Prometheus and Grafana for central-

ized monitoring and alerting.

3. **Document Versioning Strategy**: Define and implement a clear versioning strategy for the APIs.

4. **Manage Deprecation and Retirement**: Establish processes for deprecating and retiring services, including communication with stakeholders.

Conclusion

In this chapter, we explored the critical aspects of managing the lifecycle of microservices, including:

- The phases of the microservices lifecycle, from development to retirement.
- Best practices for versioning, deprecation, and retirement of services.
- Strategies for ensuring smooth transitions and minimizing disruptions.

By implementing these practices, you can effectively manage the lifecycle of your microservices, ensuring that they remain reliable, maintainable, and aligned with business needs. In the next chapter, we will delve into the future of microservices architecture, exploring emerging trends, technologies, and the evolving landscape of software development.

Chapter 14: The Future of Microservices Architecture

Microservices architecture has transformed how organizations design and build applications, enabling them to be more agile, scalable, and resilient. As technology continues to evolve, the landscape of microservices is also changing, introducing new trends and practices that promise to enhance the effectiveness of this architectural style. In this chapter, we will explore the future of microservices architecture, examining emerging technologies, evolving practices, and the potential impact of these changes on software development.

By the end of this chapter, you will have a comprehensive understanding of the trends shaping the future of microservices architecture and the opportunities they present for organizations.

Section 1: The Evolution of Microservices Architecture

1.1 Historical Context

Microservices architecture has its roots in the shift from monolithic applications to more modular, service-oriented approaches. This evolution was driven by the need for organizations to respond quickly to changing business requirements, leverage cloud computing, and adopt agile development practices.

1.2 Key Milestones in Microservices Development

- **Service-Oriented Architecture (SOA)**: The precursor to microservices, SOA emphasized reusable services and interoperability, laying the groundwork for later developments.
- **Agile Development**: The rise of agile methodologies fostered a culture of rapid iteration and continuous improvement, promoting the adoption of microservices.
- **Cloud Computing**: The advent of cloud services provided the scalability and flexibility necessary for deploying and managing microservices.

1.3 Current State of Microservices

Today, microservices architecture is widely adopted across industries, enabling organizations to develop, deploy, and scale applications more efficiently. The current state of microservices is characterized by:

- A focus on DevOps practices to streamline development and operations.
- Increased use of containerization technologies (e.g., Docker, Kubernetes) to manage microservices deployments.
- Adoption of API gateways and service meshes to enhance communication and management between services.

Section 2: Emerging Trends in Microservices Architecture

2.1 Serverless Computing

Serverless computing abstracts the underlying infrastructure management, allowing developers to focus on writing code without worrying about server provisioning and scaling. In a serverless architecture, code is executed in response to events, with the cloud provider automatically managing resource allocation.

Benefits of Serverless Computing

- **Cost Efficiency**: Pay only for the compute resources used during

function execution, reducing costs associated with idle resources.

- **Scalability**: Automatically scale to accommodate varying workloads without manual intervention.
- **Faster Time to Market**: Accelerate development cycles by allowing developers to concentrate on writing business logic.

Use Cases in Microservices

Microservices can leverage serverless architectures for specific tasks, such as:

- Processing asynchronous events (e.g., from message queues).
- Executing background jobs and scheduled tasks.
- Implementing APIs and microservices that respond to HTTP requests.

2.2 Microservices Mesh

A **microservices mesh** is an architectural pattern that provides a dedicated infrastructure layer for managing service-to-service communications. This layer can handle service discovery, load balancing, traffic management, security, and observability.

Key Components of a Microservices Mesh

1. **Service Discovery**: Automatically detects and manages service instances in the network.
2. **Traffic Management**: Controls traffic routing and load balancing, allowing for canary releases and blue-green deployments.
3. **Security**: Enforces policies for authentication, authorization, and encryption of service communications.
4. **Observability**: Provides metrics, logging, and tracing capabilities to monitor the health and performance of services.

Tools for Implementing a Microservices Mesh

- **Istio**: A popular service mesh that provides advanced traffic management, security, and observability features for microservices.

- **Linkerd**: A lightweight service mesh focused on simplicity and performance, providing essential features for managing service communications.

Section 3: Integration of AI and Machine Learning

3.1 The Role of AI/ML in Microservices

As organizations increasingly adopt AI and machine learning (ML) technologies, integrating these capabilities into microservices architecture becomes crucial. AI/ML can enhance the functionality of microservices, enabling intelligent decision-making, predictive analytics, and automation.

Use Cases for AI/ML in Microservices

- **Real-Time Analytics**: Implementing real-time data processing microservices to analyze data streams and generate insights.
- **Personalization**: Using machine learning models to provide personalized experiences for users based on their behavior and preferences.
- **Predictive Maintenance**: Leveraging AI to predict failures and optimize the maintenance of systems and services.

3.2 Building AI-Enabled Microservices

1. **Model Training and Deployment**: Train machine learning models separately and deploy them as microservices. This allows for easy scaling and updating of models without impacting other services.
2. **Data Pipelines**: Create dedicated microservices for data ingestion, processing, and transformation, ensuring that the data used for training and inference is reliable and up-to-date.
3. **API Integration**: Expose machine learning models as APIs, allowing other microservices to consume predictions and insights seamlessly.

Section 4: Evolving DevOps Practices

4.1 The Role of DevOps in Microservices
DevOps is a set of practices that combine software development (Dev) and IT operations (Ops) to shorten the development lifecycle and deliver high-quality software. In a microservices architecture, DevOps practices are essential for managing the complexity of deploying and maintaining multiple services.
Key DevOps Practices for Microservices

1. **Continuous Integration and Continuous Deployment (CI/CD)**: Automating the build, testing, and deployment processes to enable rapid and reliable delivery of microservices.
2. **Infrastructure as Code (IaC)**: Managing infrastructure through code, allowing teams to provision and manage resources consistently across environments.
3. **Monitoring and Logging**: Implementing monitoring solutions to gain visibility into microservices performance and ensure reliability.
4. 2 Implementing DevOps in Microservices
5. **Automated Testing**: Create automated test suites for microservices to validate functionality and performance during the CI/CD process.
6. **Containerization**: Use Docker to containerize microservices, ensuring consistent environments from development to production.
7. **Orchestration**: Leverage Kubernetes or similar orchestration tools to manage the deployment, scaling, and operation of microservices.

Section 5: Impact of Evolving Business Needs

5.1 Responding to Market Changes
As business needs evolve, microservices must be able to adapt quickly to changing requirements. Organizations must be agile and responsive to market trends, customer feedback, and competitive pressures.
Strategies for Agile Adaptation

- **Feature Flags**: Implement feature flags to enable or disable features without redeploying code. This allows teams to test new features with specific users or roll back features if necessary.
- **Modular Design**: Design microservices to be modular and composable, allowing teams to easily add, remove, or modify services based on changing needs.

5.2 Aligning Technology with Business Goals

Microservices architecture should align with business objectives, enabling organizations to achieve their goals effectively. This alignment ensures that technology choices support business strategies and enhance customer experiences.

Steps to Align Technology and Business

1. **Regular Stakeholder Engagement**: Involve business stakeholders in technology discussions to ensure alignment with strategic goals.
2. **Iterative Development**: Adopt agile methodologies to deliver features iteratively, allowing for adjustments based on feedback.
3. **Metrics and KPIs**: Define key performance indicators (KPIs) to measure the impact of microservices on business outcomes and ensure that technology supports growth.

Section 6: Future Considerations for Microservices

6.1 Emerging Technologies

The future of microservices architecture will be influenced by emerging technologies, including:

- **Edge Computing**: Distributing computation closer to data sources to reduce latency and improve performance for real-time applications.
- **5G Networks**: Enhancing connectivity and enabling new use cases for microservices in IoT and mobile applications.
- **Blockchain**: Providing decentralized solutions for data integrity and

trust in distributed applications.

6.2 The Shift Towards Event-Driven Architectures

Event-driven architectures will continue to gain traction in microservices, allowing services to react to events asynchronously. This approach enhances scalability and decouples services, making the architecture more resilient.

6.3 Continuous Learning and Adaptation

Organizations must foster a culture of continuous learning and adaptation, encouraging teams to experiment with new technologies, tools, and practices. This mindset will be essential for staying competitive in a rapidly changing landscape.

Section 7: Case Study: The Future of Microservices in an Organization

Let's explore a case study of an organization successfully adapting to the future of microservices architecture.

7.1 Company Overview

A leading e-commerce company has transitioned to a microservices architecture to improve scalability and agility. The company operates several microservices, including product catalog, order processing, payment, and notification services.

7.2 Implementation of Emerging Trends

1. **Serverless Computing**: The company adopted serverless functions for processing payments and sending notifications, reducing operational overhead and improving scalability.
2. **Microservices Mesh**: Implemented a service mesh to manage communication between microservices, improving observability and security.
3. **AI Integration**: Integrated machine learning models to provide personalized product recommendations, leveraging data from user interactions.

7.3 Outcomes and Benefits

- **Faster Feature Delivery**: The company reduced time-to-market for new features, enabling them to respond quickly to customer demands.
- **Improved Scalability**: The adoption of serverless and microservices mesh improved scalability and resilience during peak shopping seasons.
- **Enhanced Customer Experience**: AI-driven recommendations led to increased customer engagement and satisfaction.

Conclusion

In this chapter, we explored the future of microservices architecture, focusing on emerging trends, technologies, and evolving practices that shape the landscape. Key takeaways include:

- **The evolution of microservices** from monolithic architectures, driven by the need for agility and scalability.
- **Emerging trends** such as serverless computing, microservices mesh, and AI integration, which enhance microservices capabilities.
- **The importance of DevOps practices** in streamlining development, deployment, and operations in microservices environments.
- **Strategies for aligning technology** with evolving business needs to ensure that microservices support organizational goals.

As organizations continue to embrace microservices, staying informed about these trends and best practices will be essential for success in the ever-changing world of software development. In the next chapter, we will summarize the key concepts covered throughout this book and provide final thoughts on the journey of adopting microservices architecture.

Chapter 15: Conclusion and Key Takeaways

Microservices architecture has emerged as a transformative approach to building and managing modern applications. As organizations continue to navigate the complexities of digital transformation, the adoption of microservices enables greater agility, scalability, and resilience. In this final chapter, we will summarize the key concepts discussed throughout the book, reflect on the journey of implementing microservices, and provide actionable insights for organizations seeking to leverage this architecture.

Section 1: Recap of Key Concepts

1.1 Understanding Microservices

Microservices architecture is characterized by the decomposition of applications into smaller, independent services that communicate over well-defined APIs. This approach allows for:

- **Modularity**: Each service can be developed, deployed, and maintained independently, enabling teams to work autonomously and reduce dependencies.
- **Scalability**: Services can be scaled horizontally or vertically based on

demand, improving resource utilization and application performance.
- **Resilience**: The architecture supports fault isolation, meaning that the failure of one service does not compromise the entire application.

1.2 Design Principles

Throughout the book, we discussed essential design principles for building microservices:

- **Single Responsibility**: Each microservice should focus on a specific business capability, promoting separation of concerns.
- **Decoupling**: Services should be loosely coupled to minimize dependencies and enable independent development and deployment.
- **API-First Approach**: Designing APIs upfront ensures that services can communicate effectively and provides clarity for consumers.

1.3 Implementation Strategies

Successful implementation of microservices requires a well-defined strategy, including:

- **CI/CD Pipelines**: Automating the build, testing, and deployment processes to ensure rapid and reliable delivery of services.
- **Monitoring and Observability**: Implementing monitoring solutions to gain insights into service performance and health.
- **Resilience Patterns**: Utilizing patterns like Circuit Breaker, Retry, and Fallback to enhance service resilience and fault tolerance.

1.4 Managing Data Consistency

Managing data consistency in a distributed environment is one of the critical challenges in microservices:

- **Saga Pattern**: The Saga pattern enables managing distributed transactions across microservices, ensuring data integrity while allowing for eventual consistency.

- **CQRS**: Command Query Responsibility Segregation separates read and write operations, optimizing performance and scalability.

Section 2: Reflecting on the Microservices Journey

2.1 The Adoption Process

The journey to adopting microservices architecture typically involves several phases:

- **Assessment**: Organizations must assess their current architecture, identifying the need for transformation and potential benefits of microservices.
- **Planning**: A clear plan is essential for defining the scope, goals, and timeline for the transition.
- **Incremental Implementation**: Transitioning to microservices should be done incrementally, starting with less critical services to minimize risk.

2.2 Overcoming Challenges

Organizations may encounter several challenges during their microservices journey, including:

- **Cultural Shifts**: Moving from a monolithic mindset to a microservices approach requires changes in team structure, collaboration, and communication.
- **Complexity Management**: The complexity of managing multiple services can lead to operational challenges. Implementing robust DevOps practices and automation is crucial.
- **Service Discovery and Management**: As the number of services grows, efficiently managing service discovery, load balancing, and communication becomes essential.

2.3 Learning and Adaptation

Throughout the journey, organizations should foster a culture of learning and adaptation:

- **Continuous Improvement**: Regularly evaluate processes, tools, and technologies to identify opportunities for improvement.
- **Feedback Loops**: Establish feedback mechanisms to gather insights from users and stakeholders, ensuring that services meet their needs.

Section 3: Key Takeaways

3.1 Start Small, Scale Gradually

When adopting microservices, begin with a small, manageable subset of services. This approach allows teams to gain experience and learn from early implementations before scaling to more complex services.

3.2 Focus on Business Value

Align microservices development with business objectives. Prioritize features and services that deliver the most value to users and stakeholders, ensuring that technology supports strategic goals.

3.3 Prioritize Security and Compliance

Security should be integrated into every phase of the microservices lifecycle. Adopt best practices for securing services, including authentication, authorization, and data protection.

3.4 Embrace Automation

Automation is key to managing the complexity of microservices. Implement CI/CD pipelines, automated testing, and monitoring to streamline development and ensure consistent quality.

3.5 Invest in Observability

Implement robust monitoring and observability practices to gain insights into service performance and health. Use tools like Prometheus and Grafana to visualize metrics and facilitate troubleshooting.

3.6 Cultivate a Collaborative Culture

Encourage collaboration between development and operations teams (DevOps) to break down silos and foster a shared understanding of service management and deployment.

Section 4: The Future of Microservices Architecture

4.1 Emerging Technologies

As technology continues to evolve, new trends and technologies will shape the future of microservices architecture:

- **Serverless Computing**: The rise of serverless computing will provide more options for executing microservices without managing infrastructure.
- **Service Meshes**: Service meshes will become increasingly important for managing service-to-service communication and enhancing observability and security.

4.2 AI and Machine Learning Integration

The integration of AI and machine learning capabilities into microservices will enable intelligent decision-making and enhance service functionality, leading to more personalized and responsive applications.

4.3 Continuous Evolution

Microservices architecture is not a static solution but rather a continuously evolving paradigm. Organizations must stay informed about emerging trends, tools, and practices to remain competitive and effectively meet the needs of their users.

Section 5: Final Thoughts

Adopting microservices architecture is a significant undertaking that requires careful planning, execution, and ongoing management. While the journey may present challenges, the benefits of increased agility, scalability, and resilience make it a worthwhile investment for organizations seeking to thrive in the digital age.

By embracing the principles and practices outlined in this book, organizations can successfully navigate the complexities of microservices architecture and unlock its full potential. The future of microservices is bright, and as technology continues to advance, so too will the opportunities for innovation and growth.

Conclusion

In this final chapter, we have reflected on the key concepts covered throughout the book and explored the journey of adopting microservices architecture. As organizations continue to evolve in the face of changing business needs and technological advancements, managing the lifecycle of microservices will be essential for success.

Thank you for joining this exploration of microservices architecture. We hope this knowledge empowers you to build, manage, and innovate with microservices in your organization, paving the way for a more agile and resilient future.

Conclusion

As we wrap up our exploration of microservices architecture, it is essential to reflect on the key insights and practices discussed throughout the book. The journey to adopting and implementing microservices is not merely a technological shift but a comprehensive transformation that can redefine how organizations operate, develop software, and interact with their customers. This conclusion synthesizes the fundamental concepts, practical strategies, and future considerations surrounding microservices, providing a roadmap for success.

Embracing the Microservices Paradigm

The shift from monolithic architectures to microservices represents a significant evolution in software development. By breaking applications into smaller, independent services, organizations can achieve greater agility and flexibility. This modular approach enables teams to work autonomously, adopt faster release cycles, and respond more swiftly to changing business demands.

Key takeaways include:

- **Modularity**: Each microservice is designed to fulfill a specific business capability, allowing teams to develop, deploy, and maintain services independently. This separation of concerns simplifies the development process and enhances the ability to adapt to changes.

- **Scalability**: Microservices can be scaled horizontally, allowing organizations to manage workloads efficiently and ensure that applications can handle fluctuating traffic without sacrificing performance.
- **Resilience**: By isolating services, microservices architectures improve fault tolerance. The failure of one service does not impact the entire application, enabling a more reliable user experience.

Best Practices for Implementation

Throughout the book, we have discussed essential best practices for implementing microservices, emphasizing the importance of strategic planning, development, deployment, and operations. The following practices stand out as vital for successful microservices adoption:

1. **Start Small, Scale Gradually**: Organizations should begin by identifying non-critical services to convert into microservices. This incremental approach allows teams to learn and iterate before tackling more complex applications.
2. **Adopt CI/CD Pipelines**: Implementing continuous integration and continuous deployment pipelines automates testing and deployment, reducing errors and improving release velocity. This practice fosters a culture of automation and collaboration, enabling teams to deliver high-quality software consistently.
3. **Ensure Security**: Security should be integrated throughout the microservices lifecycle. By adopting best practices for authentication, authorization, and data protection, organizations can mitigate risks and protect sensitive information.
4. **Implement Monitoring and Observability**: Establishing robust monitoring solutions is crucial for maintaining service health. By leveraging tools such as Prometheus and Grafana, organizations can gain insights into performance, detect anomalies, and respond proactively to potential issues.

5. **Versioning and Deprecation Management**: Managing the lifecycle of microservices includes implementing versioning strategies and preparing for deprecation. Organizations should communicate changes clearly and provide migration paths to ensure a smooth transition for users.

The Role of Emerging Technologies

As the landscape of software development continues to evolve, several emerging technologies will shape the future of microservices architecture:

- **Serverless Computing**: This model abstracts infrastructure management, allowing developers to focus on writing code. Microservices can leverage serverless functions for specific tasks, such as event processing, improving scalability and cost-effectiveness.
- **Service Mesh**: A service mesh provides a dedicated layer for managing service-to-service communications, enabling features such as load balancing, security, and observability. This approach simplifies complex microservices interactions, enhancing reliability.
- **AI and Machine Learning**: Integrating AI and machine learning capabilities into microservices will enable organizations to create intelligent applications that can analyze data, make predictions, and automate processes.

Continuous Learning and Adaptation

Adopting microservices architecture is not a one-time effort; it requires a culture of continuous learning and adaptation. Organizations must remain vigilant in evaluating their processes, tools, and technologies, ensuring that they evolve alongside changing business needs and technological advancements.

- **Feedback Loops**: Establish mechanisms to gather feedback from users and stakeholders, allowing for iterative improvements based on real-world experiences.

- **Agile Mindset**: Foster an agile mindset across teams, encouraging experimentation and innovation while being open to change.

Final Thoughts

The journey into microservices architecture can be complex, yet the rewards are substantial. By embracing the principles and practices outlined in this book, organizations can harness the full potential of microservices to build resilient, scalable, and high-quality applications.

As you move forward, keep in mind that the future of microservices is not just about technology; it's about transforming how teams collaborate, how businesses operate, and how customers experience your products and services. By prioritizing agility, quality, and innovation, organizations can thrive in an increasingly digital landscape.

www.ingramcontent.com/pod-product-compliance
Lightning Source LLC
LaVergne TN
LVHW051333050326
832903LV00031B/3509